DEDICATION:

To the greatest in-laws in the world, Gwen and Winfield Lawrence, along with my thanks to:

Paul Mayer, for introducing me to the wonderful world of fine cuisine;
Joyce Elder with her ever-ready typewriter;
that unbelievable redhead, Bernice Jiminez, who introduced me to that
most charming man in all San Francisco, Fire Chief William F. Murray,
who knows more about San Francisco than anyone;
and for
the "whole bunch" of love of three beautiful children, Becky Joy, Bob, Jr., and Bill, and
the most patient, understanding, and wonderful husband in the world.

Barbara Lawrence

Fisherman's Wharf cookbook

By Barbara Lawrence

Illustrations by Mike Nelson

© 1971
Nitty Gritty Productions
Concord, California

A Nitty Gritty Book*
Published by
Nitty Gritty Productions
P.O. Box 5457
Concord, California 94524

*Nitty Gritty Books - Trademark
Owned by Nitty Gritty Productions
Concord, California

ISBN 0-911954-13-9
Library of Congress Catalog Card Number: 79-30867

books designed with giving in mind

Pies & Cakes
Yogurt
The Ground Beef Cookbook
Cocktails & Hors d'Oeuvres
Salads & Casseroles
Kid's Party Book
Pressure Cooking
Food Processor Cookbook
Peanuts & Popcorn
Kid's Pets Book
Make It Ahead
    French Cooking
Soups & Stews
Crepes & Omelets

Microwave Cooking
Vegetable Cookbook
Kid's Arts and Crafts
Bread Baking
The Crockery Pot Cookbook
Kid's Garden Book
Classic Greek Cooking
Low Carbohydrate Cookbook
Kid's Cookbook
Italian
Cheese Guide & Cookbook
Miller's German
Quiche & Souffle
To My Daughter, With Love

Natural Foods
Chinese Vegetarian
The Jewish Cookbook
Working Couples
Mexican
Sunday Breakfast
Fisherman's Wharf Cookbook
Charcoal Cookbook
Ice Cream Cookbook
Blender Cookbook
The Wok, a Chinese Cookbook
Japanese Country
Fondue Cookbook

from nitty gritty productions

CONTENTS

FOREWORD

It is a most enjoyable experience to research a book such as this, especially when it was absolutely essential to dine in each of the restaurants whose owners so graciously assisted us in compiling this selection of seafood recipes. I found out something beautiful with seafood. You can have it every single night of the year yet never duplicate a single evening's repast.

When I told my husband that I was going to do a book on seafood, he was dubious. He said, "All seafood restaurants serve the same seafood dishes." But we found it wasn't true. For instance, bouillabaisse can be prepared in any number of ways. We have included three variations of this classic soup stew, each of which is completely different from the other. I don't think that there are any two dishes prepared exactly alike in any two restaurants. And that is because each chef is like an artist; he puts his own masterful touches to his works of art: his cuisine.

And this should be the way you attack a recipe. Don't be limited by the ingredients (but don't go overboard)! Sole en Papillote can be made with turbot as well; the squid dishes can be made with baby octopus; cannelloni can be stuffed with a variety of fish; and the Sweet and Sour Snapper recipe can be used equally well with rock cod or carp. In other words, you can be an artist, too. Don't be afraid to be inventive - but try any new recipe out on your immediate family before you prepare it for a dinner party. "They" say that artists aren't appreciated until after their demise. So be artistic, but don't carry it too far.

We have tried to be helpful by indicating the type of wine we prefer with each entree, but this of course is more of a guideline, and the wines we have chosen are from California's own vineyards. Let your own taste buds be your guide and here, again, be adventuresome. There is a lovely thrill of expectancy in buying a new kind of wine. Do keep a record on the recipes of any new discoveries that you make - in substituting ingredients and in wine preferences - for future references. You'll find this a big help (if you don't do it already).

To each of you who is patient enough to read thus far, I extend my personal good wishes for fine wining and dining. And I hope that this book will lead to a greater appreciation by others of your culinary artistry.

THE INCOMPARABLE FISHERMAN'S WHARF

San Francisco offers a wide variety of sights to see. An all-time favorite with visitors and residents alike is the incomparable Fisherman's Wharf.

A ride from the center of town on a famous cable car will carry you on a jolting ride up the steep hills, past elegant mansions, down into Chinatown, around North Beach, "Little Italy," and finally down to the wharf itself.

Fisherman's Wharf has an indefinable appeal that makes it as attractive by night as it is by day. Overhead, seagulls squeal and swoop, keeping an ever-watchful eye open for some fishy tidbit that might be tossed or thrown for them to enjoy.

In the distance you can see a ship destined for a faraway port as it glides through the golden gateway to the Pacific. Dove-grey fog creeps silently in from the ocean, past the hills of lush Marin, covering sleeping Tamalpais and all with a blanket of soft mist.

The crisp sea air of the wharf mixes with the heady aroma of boiling sidewalk crab pots, huge cauldrons that are constantly being fed from crates of fresh, squirming crabs, serving up the bright orange succulent beauties to waiting customers, some of whom hurry away to enjoy this sweet delicacy on an adjoining dock, along with a bottle of cool California wine.

Sun-browned street vendors also purvey fresh "walk-away" seafood cocktails of crab, shrimp, or oysters, served complete with tiny oyster crackers, lemon slices, and a zesty sauce, to be devoured as you stroll.

And there are cases exhibiting fresh fish for sale, fresh salmon (buy a whole one if you like) that have probably been caught that morning, squid, swordfish, lobsters, and every manner of fruits of the mighty Pacific.

What scene could be better set for a concentration of the best seafood restaurants in the world? Most of them can be observed from a vantage point in the middle of the wharf area. Others have been founded in the older parts of the City, when the wharf was still a commercial fishing boat area.

The colorful rustic planking of the piers creaks and groans with the movements of commercial and party boats, some of which are nestled between the restaurants that seem to hover on stilts over the water. The boats still come in to dock and unload and sell their catches, but the major portion of Fisherman's Wharf is now devoted to the constant stream of gourmands seeking the special cuisine the wharf is noted for. All manner of fish and shellfish are prepared by masterful chefs each of whom has his personalized interpretation of the best way to prepare them. Some of the recipes have been handed down from father to son for generations, and hark back to the sunny slopes of Italy, where the forebears of Scoma, Sabella, Geraldi, La Torre, Di Maggio, Castagnola, Pompei, Alioto, and other wharf notables, went to sea before their offspring embarked for the New World.

Until the mid-1920s Fisherman's Wharf was a major fish market, and it was shortly thereafter that some of the fishermen realized the potential that existed there for fresh-cooked seafood. Restaurants cropped up first as sidewalk stands, then — as business grew — to indoor sit-down cafes, and, finally, to elegant establishments offering the finest in seafood cuisine, including favorite Italian entrees as well as standard items to please any palate.

Though the wharf is busiest during crab season, from November to June, the popularity of all seafood has so grown that the wharf is busy year 'round, boasting a minimum of a dozen excellent such restaurants, along with other such tourist-tempting devices as the Wax Museum, Ripley's Believe-It-Or-Not Museum, wine-tasting rooms, a row of telescopes from which one can view Alcatraz Island, Tamalpais, Sausalito, or an in-coming Harbor Queen, which takes sightseers on extensive tours of the Bay.

The mystique of Fisherman's Wharf is overpowering in the evening when the

fog starts rolling in from the Bay. If you try to peer through the billowy haze you can almost see the myriad of ships once moored there during the early days of the Gold Rush, some deserted by their crews who jumped ship and went pounding up to the gold country in search of their fortunes, others still loaded with goods from the Orient, the captains desperately trying to salvage and sell the precious cargos still in the holds.

Some shipowners were still stranded on their boats when the filling-in of

water lots began, but found that they could have a wooden pile driven on either side of the ship to steady it, enabling them to sell their shiploads from the deck. They would then rent the empty hulls. Many such vessels became saloons, hotels, and houseboats. Others were sunk on site, becoming fill-in for the area. It is strange to reflect that under much of the present-day waterfront lie the graves of many sailing ships of the Gold Rush fleet. Walk softly, lest you disturb them.

Located as it is in a city that is surrounded by water on three sides, Fisherman's Wharf has always offered a magnificent view, although in recent years it has changed somewhat. Reflections in the surrounding waters and the gentle Bay fog are still there. But now, two Bay-spanning bridges tower above, while fussy little tugboats ponderously put ships of the world in their places.

West of the wharf has changed too. Little did Mr. D. Ghirardelli dream when he came from the small town of Hornitos, Italy, that his chocolate factory would one day become the sanctuary for colorful restaurants, shops, galleries, and a theater. A pre-earthquake cannery just down the street has been renovated to house a similar complex.

The San Francisco Maritime Museum, with ships models, figureheads, and ships gear of long ago, on display for the sailing buffs, is located on down the street past the wharf area on Aquatic Park, at the foot of Polk Street. Here you can also see the tiny "Mermaid" that was sailed from Japan to San Francisco in 1962.

Most of the old-timers of the wharf, along with old traditions, have passed on now. Boats are still painted blue and white in honor of "La Madonna de Luma," the fishermen's patron saint, and many fishermen and their families still solemnly participate in the blessing of the fleet on the first Sunday in October.

Gone, however, are the rugged men who worked alone against the elements for a day's catch from the sea, replaced now by younger men with new ideas and modern equipment.

We thank them and their cohorts for their gracious cooperation in helping us compile for you this book of outstanding recipes from Fisherman's Wharf and its environs.

Alioto's No. 8

Until the mid-1920s, Fisherman's Wharf was simply a wharf where fishermen brought their catch to be sold. It was in 1925 that a friend persuaded Mr. Nunzio Alioto to serve crab and shrimp cocktails in paper cups. The original stand-up counter served refreshments to early-morning fishermen heading out to sea, along with Roaring-'20s flappers heading home with their dates after a night on the town.

That tiny stand expanded to accommodate World's Fair visitors from Treasure Island across the way, and has since become a two-story showplace which offers, along with excellent food, an unequaled view of bobbing fishing boats, and bridges spanning the water to Marin County and the East Bay.

Green-vested waiters hustle back and forth across the lush red carpet, tossing the tassels on their quaint knitted fisherman's caps, while "Da Batendah" (as written on the cash register) rings up sales in the shell-decorated lounge.

Fish and shellfish are the highlights of the menu. Crab Mornay, specialty of the house, is prepared with a rich cream sauce. Delicious!

 **CANNELLONI**

First make the pancakes:

1/8 t salt	3 eggs
1 cup flour	2 t melted butter
1 cup milk	Cooking oil

Put the salt and flour into a mixing bowl. Stir in the milk, a little at a time. Add the eggs, mixing after the addition of each one. Add melted butter and mix well. Allow to sit for 1 hour.

Heat a 5-inch crepe or omelette pan. Cover the bottom of pan with oil, (about 1 T should do it), and turn heat high. Pour off excess oil, and pour in about 1 T pancake batter. Tip pan to allow batter to coat bottom evenly.

As soon as one side is golden brown, turn pancake, using a spatula. Allow to cook on second side about 1/2 minute, then turn pancake out on a plate. Repeat until all batter has been used. Now make the following filling.

1/2 pound crabmeat, cooked
2 T butter
1/2 small onion, minced
2 T parsley
2 T Parmesan cheese

Dash cayenne pepper
1 cup cream sauce (see page 154)
1 small can tomato sauce
10 pancakes
(about 5 inches in diameter)

Saute onions in butter and add crab, parsley, Parmesan cheese, pepper, and half of the cream sauce. Heat just until all ingredients have warmed through. Remove from heat, and spoon a small amount of the mixture into the center of pancake. Roll pancake and place in a shallow, buttered baking dish. Repeat until all pancakes have been used.

Combine remaining cream sauce with tomato sauce and pour over top of pancakes. Sprinkle with additional Parmesan cheese and bake in 375° oven for 20 minutes, or until heated through.

Dry Semillon

SHELLFISH BOUILLABAISSE

3 T olive oil
1 onion, chopped
1/2 cup celery, chopped
1 clove garlic, minced
Pinch of rosemary
3 ounces lobster meat, uncooked
3 ounces scallops, uncooked
4 ounces prawns, uncooked
2 ounces crab legs, shelled

4 ounces clams, raw
2 T dry Sherry
1 cup tomato pulp
1/2 lemon, sliced thinly
2 cups fish stock   (see page 154)
1 T sugar
2 T salt
1/4 t cayenne pepper
3/4 t saffron

Make fish stock. Place the olive oil in a heavy saucepan and add the onion, celery, garlic, parsley, and rosemary. Saute for 5 minutes. Then add the shellfish, all uncooked but cleaned and shelled, and the Sherry. Simmer for 5 minutes. Add the tomato pulp, lemon slices, fish stock, sugar, salt and pepper. Cook on a low flame for 10 minutes. Add the saffron at the last minute, stir well, and serve.

Chablis

FRIED OYSTERS

24 large oysters, shucked
2 eggs
1/2 t salt
1/2 t cayenne

1/2 t white pepper
1 cup milk
2 cups bread crumbs
Tartar Sauce (see page 153)

Drain oysters. Beat eggs with salt, cayenne, and pepper; add milk, and mix. Dip oysters into egg mixture, then into crumbs. Let stand 5 minutes before frying.

Fry in hot, deep fat (to 350°) until golden brown. Serve at once with Tartar Sauce.

Chablis

SCAMPI

1 pound green shrimp
1/2 cup flour
1/4 t salt
Dash pepper
2 T olive oil
2 shallots, minced

1 t lemon juice
2 T butter
1/2 cup white wine
2 T brown gravy (canned)
Chopped parsley

Peel and clean shrimp. Heat olive oil in skillet. Sprinkle the shrimp with flour and drop the floured shrimp into the hot oil. Sprinkle shrimp with salt and pepper. Allow shrimp to cook quickly, about 3 minutes, or until pink. Lower heat and drain excess olive oil. Add butter, shallots, lemon juice, white wine, and brown gravy. Allow to heat through. Top with chopped parsley and serve with steamed rice.

Johannisberg Riesling

STUFFED TURBOT WITH BONNE FEMME SAUCE

1 cup cream sauce (see page 154)
  mixed with 3 egg yolks
4 turbot fillets
1 whole green onion, chopped
1/4 pound mushrooms, chopped
1/2 cup Sherry

2 t Worcestershire sauce
1/4 cup Parmesan cheese
Salt and pepper
Paprika
2 T melted butter

Pour a layer of cream sauce in a shallow casserole. Combine onions, mushrooms, and cheese, and spread evenly in a thin layer over each fillet. Sprinkle with salt and pepper. Roll each fillet and set into casserole, rolled side down. Top each roll with 1 T Sherry and 1/2 t of Worcestershire sauce. Cover all with remaining cream sauce, and sprinkle with paprika. Pour melted butter over entire top of casserole and bake, uncovered, for 20 minutes in a 400° oven.

Riesling

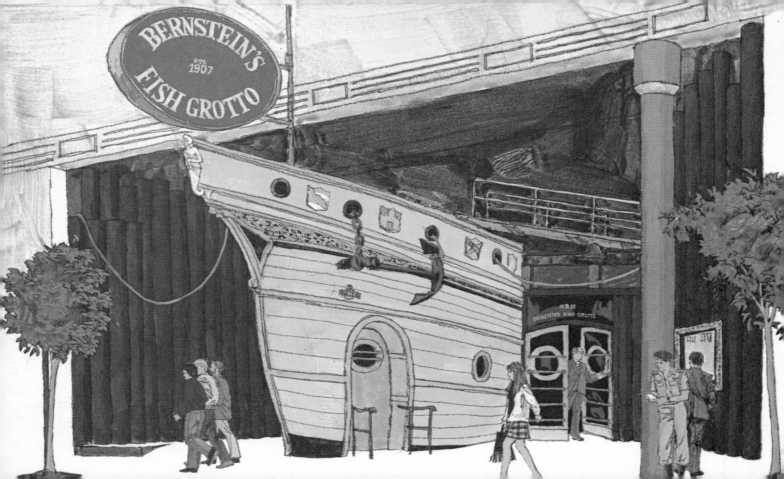

Bernstein's

Bernstein's could be considered the jumping-off spot to Fisherman's Wharf, since the cable cars clang by on their way up steep Powell Street to the top of the cliff overlooking the wharf area, then coast down - brakes always on - to the wharf itself.

As you are welcomed "aboard" the ship-like entry, you are about to begin a gastronomic voyage, served in the burnished-wood interior with deep black leather booths, or linen-covered tables surrounded by captain's chairs, under a vaulted ceiling past which you can see rigging on the next deck. Bronze lighthouses, a binnacle, panels of brilliantly-colored fish, and other ship's treasures collected from around the globe adorn the hold, presided over by a bronzed mermaid who formerly guided another Spanish Galleon. Skipper Richard Bernstein is at the helm of this San Francisco landmark, founded by his father in 1907.

The vast menu features elegant seafood, among which the Coo-Coo clam, a native of Coos Bay, Oregon, has gained great popularity. Some clam specialties are included here, and local varieties can be used in their preparation.

BISQUE

2 dozen clams
2 cups clam liquid
5 T flour
1 t salt
1/8 t pepper

1/2 cup celery, diced
2 T parsley, chopped
2 T butter
1 cup thin cream
1 cup milk

Chop the clams finely. Strain the liquid through cheesecloth, and add enough water to make 2 cups. Cook clams, celery, parsley, and liquid together for 10 minutes. Press through a sieve and keep hot.

Melt butter; add flour, salt, and pepper, and mix to smooth paste. Add cream and milk and bring to a boil, stirring constantly. Add strained clam liquid.

Serve immediately.

Folle Blanche

CLAM FRITTERS

1 dozen clams, minced
1/4 cup clam liquid
2 eggs, beaten
1/4 cup milk
1 t melted butter
1/8 t pepper
1/4 t salt
1 cup flour
Cooking butter

Sift flour, salt, and pepper. Add clam liquid, milk, and eggs. Mix all until smooth. Add butter and clams. Drop this mixture by tablespoon into hot fat (360⁰), and fry until brown.

Serve with Tartar Sauce. (See page 153)

Dry Sauvignon Blanc

COO-COO CLAM CHOWDER

1 quart shucked clams
4 cups potatoes, cut in cubes
1 1/2-inch cube of salt-pork fat
1 sliced onion
2 T flour
1 t salt
1/8 t pepper
4 T butter
4 cups scalded milk
8 crackers

Clean clams, using 1 cup cold water; drain, reserve liquid, heat it to boiling point and strain.

Chop hard part of clams very fine. Cut pork fat into small pieces and fry; add onions, fry 5 minutes, and strain into stew pan.

20

Parboil potatoes in boiling water for 5 minutes. Drain and put layer of potatoes in bottom of stew pan. Add chopped clams, sprinkle with salt, pepper, and generously with flour. Add remaining potatoes, again sprinkle with salt, pepper, and flour. Add 2 1/2 cups boiling water. Cook 10 minutes, add milk, soft part of clams, and 3 T butter. Boil 3 minutes and add crackers (split and soaked in enough cold milk to moisten). Reheat clam water to boiling point and thicken with 1 T butter and flour cooked together; add to chowder just before serving.

Note: The clam water has a tendency to cause the milk to curdle, hence it must be added last.

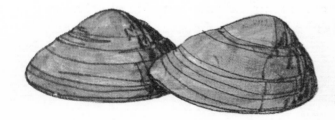

Dry Sauterne

21

COO-COO CLAMS, CHATHAM STYLE

24 large clams in their shells
2 T butter
1 T flour
1 t minced parsley
12 thin-sliced bacon strips
1 lemon, sliced
Salt and pepper

Clean and steam clams for 5 minutes. Take the clams out of shells, and remove hard parts. Strain the juice.

Prepare the sauce with butter, flour, and clam juice. Season and add parsley. Put 2 clams in each shell, cover with 1 T sauce. Top with bacon, and brown in 500° oven.

Serve with lemon wedges.

Pinot Chardonnay

DEVILED COO-COO CLAMS

3 dozen large hard-shell clams
1 cup water
1 cup dry white wine
4 T butter
1/2 cup green onions, chopped
4 shallots, minced
4 T celery, chopped

2 t dry mustard
2 cups dry bread crumbs
2 cups hot milk
2 t Worcestershire sauce
1/8 t Tabasco sauce
1 t salt
1/2 cup grated Parmesan cheese

Scrub the clams. Place them in a saucepan with the water and wine. Bring to a boil and cook until shells open. Remove clams, reserving shells. Cut off the necks of the clams and discard; coarsely chop the clams.

Melt the butter in a saucepan; saute the green onions, celery, and shallots for 5 minutes. Blend in the mustard and bread crumbs. Gradually add the milk, then the Worcestershire sauce, Tabasco sauce, salt, and clams. Fill the shells and sprinkle with cheese. Bake in a 375° oven for 5 minutes. Serve hot.

Chablis

FRIED COO-COO CLAMS

1 pint clams
Salt
Pepper
1 egg
2 T milk
Bread crumbs
Butter

Dry clams with a towel. Sprinkle them with salt and pepper.
Beat the egg with the milk.
Dip clams first in crumbs, then in egg mixture, then in crumbs.
Fry in butter which has been heated to 390°.
Drain, keep hot, and serve with Tartar Sauce (see page 153).

Chenin Blanc

DEVILED FISH LAVENGRO

6 slices bacon
1 green pepper, seeded and diced
2 T onion, minced
2 cups whole, peeled tomatoes and juice,
  (canned or fresh)
1/4 t powdered cloves

2 cups cold, cooked halibut
6 olives, sliced
1 cup bread crumbs
Butter

Fry bacon until crisp; remove from pan and crumble. Set aside.

Saute green pepper and onion in bacon fat for 2 minutes. Add tomatoes and juice, cloves, (taste for salt if desired), and allow to boil for 5 minutes. Add flaked fish, olives, and crumbled bacon. Place in a buttered ramekin, cover with bread crumbs, and dot with a little butter.

Bake in a 400° oven for 5 minutes, or until crumbs brown. Serve at once.

26   Grignolino

LOBSTER PRINCESS

1 whole lobster, cooked
1/4 t salt
1/8 t pepper
Dash cayenne
4 T butter
1 T shallots, minced

2 T Sherry
1/2 T prepared mustard
1/2 cup cream sauce (see page 154)
2 egg yolks, beaten slightly with 1 T cream
1 whole artichoke heart, chopped
Grated Parmesan cheese

Split lobster into halves. Remove meat, taking care not to crack or break shell halves. Cut meat into pieces. Melt butter in skillet and add lobster meat. Season with salt, pepper, and cayenne, and allow to saute for 2 or 3 minutes.

Add shallots and immediately add wine, mustard, and cream sauce. Simmer for about one minute. Remove from heat. Add egg yolks and cream mixture. Mix well. Stir in chopped artichoke hearts and spoon mixture evenly into two lobster shells. Sprinkle with grated cheese and bake in 425° oven until top is slightly glazed.

Serve at once.

Pinot Chardonnay

Di Maggio's

In 1937, Joseph Di Maggio, Sr., a long-time San Francisco fisherman, opened a small restaurant on the wharf. During World War II he expanded it into a night club. As his famous son, Joltin' Joe Di Maggio, slugged his way into baseball's Hall of Fame, business soared, and Di Maggio's San Francisco restaurant became one of the city's favorite dining spots.

Di Maggio brothers Dominic and Vince also attained baseball fame, and the latter is now co-owner with brother Tom of the busy restaurant.

The wide variety of offerings in the menu is as international as the Di Maggio reputation. You can find Alaskan Cod, Australian Lobster, Louisiana Shrimp, Eastern Oysters, Oregon Coo-Coo Clams, Hawaiian Mahi Mahi, and imported cheeses, to name a few. But a regular favorite is Di Maggio's own Bouillabaisse, "Fisherman's Style," for the natives and tourists alike. Serving of this dish is preceded by the ritual of the waiter's tieing a huge bib around the neck of the customer. Extra attentions to the diners and to the dinners, spell success here.

BAKED SEA BASS WITH SHRIMP SAUCE

3 fillets of sea bass
2 ounces butter
1 ounce olive oil
1 T flour

1 cup milk
2 ounces dry white wine
1 cup small shrimp
Salt and pepper

First make the sauce. Put the butter and olive oil in a small saucepan. When melted and hot, add approximately 1 T flour, and stir with a wire whisk over a low flame for 3 to 4 minutes. This roux should be smooth and not lumpy; if it is, this can be rectified by adding a little more oil or flour, whichever it may require.

When smooth, add 1 cup of warm milk, stirring constantly, until the sauce is smooth and creamy. Add salt and pepper to taste, cook about 2 minutes, then add the dry white wine, blending it in well.

Place the fillet of sea bass in a shallow baking dish, and sprinkle with the small shrimp. Cover the fish and shrimp with the sauce, and place in a moderate 350° oven for 20 minutes, or until the fish is cooked.

Grenache Rose

BAKED SEA BASS WITH ITALIAN SAUCE

4 fillets of sea bass
3 T olive oil
1 medium onion , chopped
1 green pepper, minced
1 stalk celery, chopped
1 clove garlic, minced

1 can (No. 2) solid-pack tomatoes
1 t chopped parsley
1/4 t dried oregano
2 ounces dry white wine
Salt and pepper

First make the Italian sauce. Heat the olive oil in a heavy saucepan, add the onion, pepper, and celery, all shredded, and the garlic. Braise until the vegetables are slightly cooked (limp, but not brown). Then add the tomatoes, parsley, oregano, and wine, salt and pepper to taste. Cook for about 10 minutes.

Place the pieces of bass in a large baking dish, cover with the sauce, and place in a 425° oven; cook for 10 minutes.

Zinfandel

POACHED SEA BASS

4 fillets of sea bass
8 fresh oysters (shucked)
8 fresh clams (shucked)
2 cups chicken broth
1/2 cup white wine
1/2 cup heavy cream
1/8 t curry powder
Salt and pepper

Make 4 even cuts with a sharp knife almost to the center of each fillet. Alternate one oyster and then one clam in the cuts. Place fish in a large, shallow casserole and cover with broth. Bake in 400° oven for 10 minutes.

Remove casserole from oven. Drain off liquid into a saucepan. Add the wine and cream, and whip slightly, then add remaining seasonings. Cover the bass in the casserole with this sauce and return to oven for 5 minutes.

Vin Rose

BOUILLABAISSE A LA DI MAGGIO

2 T olive oil
1 clove garlic, minced
1 cup green onions, chopped
1 T parsley, chopped
1 cup fresh clam broth
1 cup dry white wine
Salt and pepper
10 raw prawns, cleaned and shelled
12 whole scallops
1 live lobster (1 pound)
14 clams in their shells

For this dish use a French pottery casserole, 8 inches in diameter and 3 inches deep, or a Pyrex glass casserole.

Heat the olive oil in the casserole over a very low flame. Add the onions and garlic. Cook slowly for 3 minutes, then add the parsley. Remove the casserole from the fire, then add the clam broth, the wine, and salt and pepper to taste. Blend well, then add the raw prawns, scallops, oysters, and clams in their shells (which have been thoroughly scrubbed), and the raw lobster, cut into 2-inch squares. The clams should be added last, on top of the other shellfish.

Cover the casserole and simmer for 15 to 20 minutes, or until the clam shells open. Serve very hot.

Chablis

CRABMEAT CASSEROLE

1/2 cup onions, finely chopped
2 T butter
2 T flour
1 cup clam juice
1 1/2 cups tomatoes, peeled and diced
1/2 cup green pepper, chopped
2 T parsley, minced
1/4 cup green olives, sliced
1 t salt
1/2 t black pepper
1/8 t thyme
2 T Worcestershire sauce
1 pound cooked crabmeat
1/4 cup soft bread crumbs
4 T melted butter

Saute the onions in butter for 2 minutes. Blend in the flour until brown. Gradually add clam juice, stirring constantly. Stir in tomatoes, green pepper, parsley, olives, salt, pepper, thyme, and mace.

Cook over low heat for 10 minutes. Add Worcestershire sauce and crabmeat. Pour into 6 individual ovenproof ramekins or one large buttered casserole. Sprinkle with bread crumbs and pour melted butter over all.

Bake in a 350° oven 15 minutes, or until golden brown.

Zinfandel Rose

JUMBO PRAWNS WITH MUSHROOMS AND ONIONS

1 T olive oil
1 T butter
20 large prawns
1/2 cup green onions, chopped
1/2 cup fresh mushrooms, sliced
Salt and pepper
2 ounces white wine

Heat the oil and butter in a heavy saute pan. Add the jumbo shrimp, which have been peeled, deveined, and split partly through the back. Stir gently for 3 to 5 minutes. Add the chopped green onions (bulbs and tops), the mushrooms, salt and pepper to taste. Cook until the prawns have changed color, and add the dry white wine. Cook 3 minutes and serve in a hot chafing dish.

Pinot Blanc

CURRIED PRAWNS

42 large prawns
1/4 pound butter
1/2 cup mushrooms, sliced thinly
1/2 t shallots, minced
1/8 t curry powder

1/2 cup onions, chopped
1/3 cup Madeira
1 egg yolk
1/2 cup fish stock

Shell the prawns and split them down the back, cleaning the dark vein as you wash and cut them halfway through. Place in a small pan and cover with cold water. Bring to a boil. Let cook 3 to 5 minutes and remove from heat. Drain.

Place butter in skillet and melt. Add shallots, curry, onions, and mushrooms. Cook gently until tender, and add the prawns and wine. Simmer for 5 minutes; add egg yolk which has been beaten with the fish stock. Cook for 2 more minutes.

Serve on hot rice, covered with sauce.

Green Hungarian

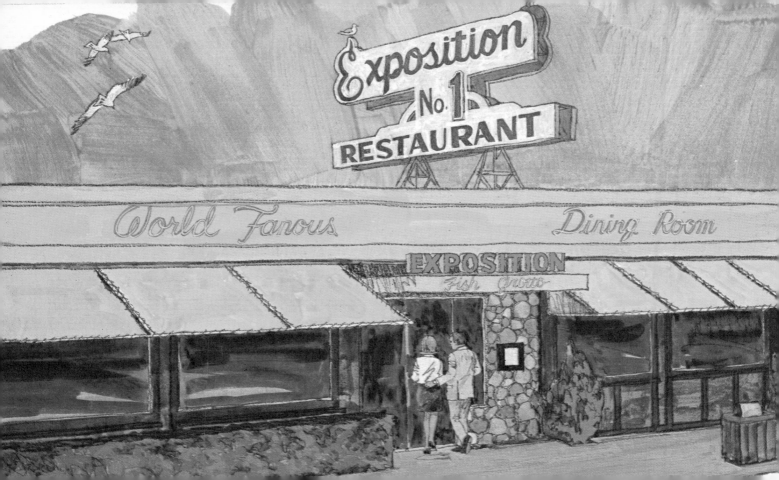

Exposition Grotto No.1

This long, low building centers in the Fisherman's Wharf area, and its claim of "No. 1" was acknowledged by the judges of the annual Crab Cooking Olympics when they gave executive chef Arthur Davis the First Award of the Crab Olympics of 1969 for the Crab Meat Mornay recipe given on the following two pages.

The mammoth dining room in Sil Oliva's popular fish grotto contains booths handsomely upholstered in rich leather. In the elegant Shell Room a huge undersea mural made from hundreds of irridescent shells reflects the soft lights, and invites pre-diners to enjoy a cocktail with their dinner companions.

A daily insert in the menu features special dishes made of seasonal catches, but the regular offerings are extensive enough to please the most demanding of gourmands.

All of which is a reflection of the old-world showmanship combined with new-world expertise that have made Exposition Grotto No. 1 a truly renowned restaurant.

41

CRAB MORNAY

Arthur W. Davis, Executive Chef, won the CRAB OLYMPICS AWARD at the 1969 Crab Olympics in San Francisco with this recipe.

BECHAMEL SAUCE: Saute one cup chopped onions, a sprig of fresh thyme, and a half teaspoon grated nutmeg, in a half pound of butter. When onions are a light transparent color, tender, but not brown, add about 1/2 cup of flour for the roux. Over very low heat, whipping constantly, add slowly a little more than a quart of cold dairy cream. Keep whipping until creamy thick. Strain and keep hot.

CRAB FUMET: You will need two crabs. Be sure to save the fat from one raw crab - this is called locally "crab butter." Put both of the cracked crabs into a steamer. Add a tablespoon of water and cover. Steam for about 15 minutes. (The crabs are cooked when the crab shells turn red.) When done, pour the broth from the cooked crabs into a cup and save. Also save and pick the meat of the crab from the shells.

To the bechamel sauce add one cup heavy cream, one cup Parmesan cheese which has been grated, one cup of soft jack cheese which has been either grated or chopped very fine and the crab "butter," which was saved from the raw crab; also add the crab fumet. Stir constantly. Add the cream slowly, never stop stirring until the cream thickens. When the cream has thickened, add 1/4 cup dry sauterne wine, salt and pepper; stir quickly. If necessary to thin the sauce a little bit, one may add a little more of the wine.

Add equal parts of crab meat and sauce. Place in a casserole. Top with grated Parmesan cheese, a small amount of paprika, then dot with butter. Place casserole in oven that has been preheated to 350°. Let bake for about 12 minutes or until the cheese browns evenly.

This recipe will make from 4 to 6 servings.

LOBSTER THERMIDOR

2 boiled lobsters
6 small green onions, chopped
6 T butter
1 cup California dry white wine
1 cup cream sauce
1/2 cup cream
1/2 t dried chervil
Salt
Dash cayenne pepper
4 T grated Parmesan cheese
Pinch dry mustard
Toasted bread crumbs
Grated Parmesan cheese
Butter

Cut the boiled lobsters in half, and remove the meat from the body (and claws if an Eastern lobster is used), and dice it.

Chop the little green onions (bulbs and tops), and saute slowly in the hot butter, but do not brown. When the onions are soft, add the white wine, and simmer until partly reduced (about 1/2). Then pour this very slowly, stirring constantly, into the cream sauce. Add the cream, the dried chervil, salt to taste, and a dash of cayenne pepper. Mix well, then remove from the flame and mix in the grated cheese and the mustard.

Combine the sauce and the lobster meat, and fill the 4 half lobster shells. Top with toasted bread crumbs mixed with grated Parmesan cheese (half and half), dot with butter, place on a baking sheet, and bake in a 375° oven for 15 to 20 minutes. Just before serving, put under the broiler to quickly brown.

Dry Semillon

BAKED ROCK COD WITH CRABMEAT

4 T butter
2 pounds rock cod fillets
1/4 cup green onions, chopped
1/4 cup shallots, chopped
1 cup tomatoes, solid-pack
1/2 cup dry white wine
3/4 cup cooked crabmeat
Salt and pepper to taste

Melt butter in an ovenproof casserole. Place rock cod in casserole and sprinkle lightly with salt and pepper. Add onions and shallots, (if you are unable to find shallots, use green onions), white wine and tomatoes. Flake crabmeat overall, and bake in a 350° oven for about 15 minutes, or until heated through.

Dry Semillon

OLYMPIA OYSTER FANCY PEPPER POT

4 T butter
1 green pepper, minced
150 Olympia oysters
2 cups tomato catsup
2 t Worcestershire sauce
Toast

    Melt the butter in a saucepan and add the green pepper. Saute for 5 minutes. Then add the oysters (all 150 of them!) and cook for 5 minutes. Then add the catsup and Worcestershire sauce, mix gently, and pour into 4 individual casserole dishes lined with toast. Serve quickly, and hot.

Folle Blanche

Fishermen's Grotto No.9

Old Italy is combined with a touch of America to provide pleasant decor at Fishermen's Gotto No. 9. On the first level you will find a delightful Venetian paradise with gaily striped mooring poles. Upstairs are a lovely Florentine cocktail lounge and a spacious dining room with a magnificent view of the wharf area.

The late Mike Geraldi and his family, carrying on his tradition, have specialized in the finest seafood available for over 37 years. At the "ripe old age" of 11 Mr. Geraldi was sorting fish for wholesalers. He was paid in fish, which he then sold for cash. From money saved he bought a fishing boat of his own.

It was just a few years later that the enterprising young man realized how few restaurants there were to take advantage of the excellent source of fish from the California coastal waters.

So it was that in 1935 Mike Geraldi built his original restaurant on Fisherman's Wharf and named it Fishermen's Grotto No. 9, an establishment whose culinary artistry as well as its trademark, "the little fisherman," are world-renowned.

BOILED HALIBUT WITH MUSTARD SAUCE

2 pounds halibut
Salt and pepper
Court bouillon
1/2 pound fresh mushrooms, sliced
5 T butter
3 T flour
3 ounces dry Sherry

1 cup milk
1 cup cream
Pinch of cayenne pepper
1 beaten egg yolk
1 T dry mustard
1 T warm water

Wash the halibut quickly in cold water, wipe dry, and sprinkle with salt and pepper. Then wrap in cheesecloth (place the fish in the center of a square of cheesecloth, gather the corners together, and tie securely with a piece of string). Place the wrapped fish in a kettle and cover with the white wine, court bouillon (see recipe on page 155). Heat until the court bouillon begins to boil, then lower the flame and simmer for 20 minutes. Then take the fish from the kettle, drain, and

50

carefully remove the cheesecloth. Place the fish on a warm serving platter and keep hot.

Saute the sliced mushrooms and the chopped onion in 2 T of butter for about 7 minutes in a saucepan.

In another saucepan melt 3 T of butter and add the flour, blending it in well. Then add the Sherry and cook gently for a few moments. Next slowly add the milk and cream (mixed), stirring constantly until all is well blended. Season with salt to taste and add the cayenne pepper. When the sauce has thickened, remove from the fire and stir in the beaten egg yolk. Then add the mustard mixed with the warm water, and when that has been blended in, pour the sauce over the boiled halibut, and serve.

Rhine Wine

BOUILLABAISSE ITALIANO

1/2 cup olive oil
1/2 cup onions, chopped
1 T garlic, chopped
1 T parsley, chopped
1 T celery, chopped
1 T green pepper, chopped
2 cups solid-pack tomatoes
2 T salt
1 T paprika

1/2 cup Sherry
3 cups water
Pinch of dried basil
2 1/2 cups crabmeat
2 1/2 pounds large shrimp
3 sea bass, cut into bite-size pieces
1/2 pound chopped lobster meat
1 1/2 pounds clams
1 cup tomato sauce

Braise the onions, garlic, parsley, celery, and green peppers in the olive oil until they are a golden brown. Then add the tomatoes and the tomato sauce, salt, pepper, paprika and Sherry. Cook 15 minutes. Add the water and the dried basil, and cook slowly for 1 hour. After the sauce is cooked and seasoned to taste, add all the seafood, and cook together for 40 minutes. Serve with lots of French bread.

Gamay

CRABMEAT CAKES ITALIENNE

1 pound fresh crabmeat
1 t garlic, minced
1 cup Parmesan cheese, grated
1 t parsley, chopped
2 whole eggs
Salt and pepper
3 T olive oil

Mix together the crabmeat, Parmesan cheese, parsley, and minced garlic. Mix in 2 lightly beaten eggs, and form this mixture into small patties. Season with salt and pepper to taste.

Heat the olive oil in a skillet, and when hot add the patties, fry on each side until golden brown. Serve hot and prepare to smack your lips!

Grenache Rose

CRAB LEGS AND SHRIMP CREOLE

1/4 cup olive oil
1/2 cup onion, chopped
1 t garlic, chopped
1 t parsley, chopped
1 t celery, chopped
1 cup solid-pack tomatoes
1 cup tomato sauce

1/4 cup Sherry
1 t pepper
1 t salt
1/2 t paprika
1 1/2 cups water
1/2 cup crab legs
1/2 cup cooked shrimp

Braise the onions, celery, garlic, and parsley in olive oil until they are golden brown. Then add the tomatoes, the tomato sauce, water, salt, pepper, and paprika. Simmer for 1 hour.

Add the Sherry and simmer for about 5 minutes. Place the crab legs and the shrimp in a buttered casserole, cover with the sauce, and bake in a moderate 350° oven for 20 minutes.

Gewurztraminer

SCALLOPS IN WINE

1 pound scallops
8 T butter
3 ounces dry white wine
1/2 pound fresh mushrooms, sliced
1/2 cup onions, chopped
3 T flour
3 ounces Sherry

1 cup cream
1 cup milk
Salt
Cayenne pepper
1 beaten egg yolk
Bread crumbs

Saute the scallops in 3 T butter until golden brown. Add the dry white wine, stirring well. Then transfer the scallops to a buttered casserole.

Saute the sliced mushrooms and the chopped onion in 2 T of butter for 7 minutes.

Melt 3 T of butter in another saucepan, and add the flour, blending it in well. Then add the Sherry and cook gently for a few minutes. Next slowly add the milk and cream (mixed), stirring constantly until all is well blended. Season with salt and a pinch of cayenne pepper. When sauce has thickened, remove from the fire, and stir in the beaten egg yolk. Pour the sauce over the scallops in the casserole, top with bread crumbs, dot with butter, and place the casserole in a preheated 350° oven for about 10 minutes, or until top is brown.

Dry Semillon

SPAGHETTI WITH CRAB

1/4 cup olive oil
1/2 cup onion, chopped
1 t garlic, chopped
1 t parsley, chopped
1 t celery, chopped
1 cup solid-pack tomatoes
1 cup tomato sauce
1/4 cup Sherry

1 t black pepper
2 t salt
1/2 t paprika
1 1/2 cups water
1 pound crabmeat
1 pound spaghetti
Grated Parmesan cheese

In a heavy saucepan, heat the olive oil, and braise the onion, garlic, celery, and parsley until golden brown. Then add the tomatoes, tomato sauce, water, and seasonings. Simmer slowly for 1 hour. Then add the crabmeat and the wine, and simmer for a few minutes until thoroughly heated.

Cook the spaghetti in boiling, salted water for 12 minutes. Drain it, and add to the sauce. Mix well, then pour on a platter, and sprinkle with cheese. Serve at once.

Barbera

SEAFOOD SALAD DRESSING

2 cups mayonnaise
1 1/2 cups chili sauce
1 t lemon juice
1 t horseradish
1/4 cup sour pickles, chopped
1/4 cup celery, chopped
1/2 t Worcestershire sauce

Mix all ingredients. When well blended, store in refrigerator in a covered jar. Serve as a dressing for any seafood salad.

Pinot Blanc

Franciscan

Presiding like a grande dame, the Franciscan sits alone on the wharf, a cluster of shops on her first floor. Carpeted steps open to the second-floor terraced restaurant on one side, and a double view of the ocean on the other side for the cocktail crowd. Mirrors behind the long bar present a kaleidoscopic view of ships going to sea, sailboats, dredges at work, harbor activities, and - in the distance - Alcatraz. A collage of San Francisco decorates the menu, which features this nostalgic poem.

SAN FRANCISCO . . . . With her hills she is Rome, With her Bay she is Naples,
With her sometimes blue sky she is Switzerland. With her fog she is London,
With her boulevards she is Paris,
With her symphony and opera she is Vienna.
With her marts of trade she is New York.
But with her people, bless them, with her people, she is just SAN FRANCISCO.

The happy Franciscan monk logo boasts, "Only our food surpasses our view." A truism, indeed.

HALIBUT FLORENTINE

4 halibut steaks
1 cup spinach, chopped*
1 cup cream sauce (see page 154)
1/2 garlic clove, minced
Dash of nutmeg
1 cup Hollandaise Sauce (see page 155)

Poach the halibut, adding a few slices of lemon to the poaching water. When cooked, arrange the steaks in a buttered, shallow, ovenproof casserole.

*Wash and cook 2 bunches of fresh spinach or cook one 10-ounce package of frozen spinach as directed on package. Drain well. Chop cooked spinach finely and add a half clove minced garlic, 1 cup medium cream sauce, and a dash of nutmeg. Cook this mixture slowly for a few minutes.

Spread spinach mixture over top of halibut steaks. Top with Hollandaise Sauce and bake in a 400° oven for 10 minutes.

Gewurztraminer

CRAB OMELETTE

1 T olive oil
1 T onion, minced
4 eggs, beaten
1 cup crabmeat, cooked
2 T grated Parmesan cheese
1 T parsley, minced
Rasher of crisp, fried bacon

In an 8-inch skillet heat olive oil over a medium heat. Add onion and saute until golden. Mix eggs, crabmeat, and cheese, and add to pan with cooked onion. Reduce the heat slightly.

As the omelet cooks lift it with a spatula, letting the uncooked part run underneath. When the top looks creamy and almost set, increase the heat to let it brown slightly underneath. Turn the omelet onto a hot plate and fold it in half. Top with a pat of butter and sprinkle with parsley. Serve with crisp, fried bacon.

Chablis

SEAFOOD A LA NEWBURG

1 1/2 pounds mixed shellfish, cooked
  (crab, shrimp, lobster, scallops)
2 cubes butter
2 cups heavy cream
1/2 t salt

Dash of cayenne
1/8 t nutmeg
2 egg yolks
2 T cream
1/4 cup Sherry

    Melt butter in large skillet. Saute mixed shellfish that has been cut into bite-size pieces. Add 2 cups cream and heat until the mixture begins to boil. Lower the heat and add the salt, cayenne, and nutmeg. Beat egg yolks with 2 T cream; add to seafood mixture. Stir until thickened but do not boil. Add Sherry and heat through.

    Serve at once on toast points.

Dry Sauterne

JUMBO SHRIMP SAUTE MARSALA

2 pounds shrimp
1/3 cup green onions, chopped
1/3 cup onion, chopped
1 small clove garlic, minced
Dash each, salt and pepper
Pinch of rosemary
1 cup brown gravy (canned may be used)
1/3 cup Marsala

Peel, slit, and wash the shrimp. Saute in red-hot pan with 2 T oil; add the onions, garlic, and rosemary. Simmer for a few minutes; add the Marsala and brown gravy; simmer for 10 minutes. Add salt and pepper.

Serve with rice pilaf.

Chablis

65

SPAGHETTI WITH CLAM SAUCE

18 large, fresh cherrystone clams
2 pounds fresh littleneck clams
2 cloves garlic, minced
1/4 cup parsley, chopped
1/4 cup olive oil
1/4 cup butter
Pinch of cayenne

1/8 t black pepper
2 large ripe tomatoes, chopped
1 T tomato paste
1 can (buffet-size) tomato sauce
1 T flour
3/4 pound spaghetti

Grated Parmesan cheese

Open cherrystone clams, saving juices, and chop, medium fine. Wash littleneck clams under running water, scrubbing them well.

Combine olive oil and butter in a skillet and melt. Add chopped clams; cook for 3 minutes. Add garlic, parsley, cayenne, and black pepper. Stir and allow to cook 2 minutes. Add tomatoes, paste, sauce, 2 T of the reserved clam juice, and flour. Add littlenecks, cover and cook 10 minutes. Sprinkle cheese and part of the sauce over cooked spaghetti; toss. Pour onto platter, spoon sauce overall, and serve.

Chianti

AVOCADO STUFFED WITH CRAB

1 large avocado
1 cup crabmeat, cooked
1/2 cup celery, diced
1 onion, grated
1 T lemon juice
1/4 cup mayonnaise
Dash of salt

4 whole crab legs, cooked
4 asparagus spears, cooked
1 boiled egg, quartered
4 ripe olives
Shredded iceberg lettuce
Paprika
1 cup Thousand Island Sauce (see page 152)

Carefully peel the avocado, then cut it in half lengthwise. Sprinkle with a little lemon juice to prevent discoloration. Set each half on a plate filled with lettuce.

Combine flaked crabmeat, celery, onion, lemon juice, and mayonnaise. Season with a dash of salt. Fill hollow of each avocado with crab mixture. Top crab mound with 1/2 cup Thousand Island Sauce and garnish each plate with 2 whole crab legs, 2 asparagus spears, and 2 quarters of hard-cooked egg. Sprinkle all with a dash of paprika, and top with 2 ripe olives.

Pinot Chardonnay

THE MANDARIN

The Mandarin

Fisherman's Wharf ends at bustling Ghirardelli Square, and it is there — in the Woolen Building — that you can find an authentic mandarin cuisine where the subtle flavors and spices of the Orient impart a different and delicious flavor to seafood.

An elevator whisks the customer from a busy first-floor shopping area to the quietude of The Mandarin restaurant, where a glistening blue-tiled hallway, bordered by carved wooden screens brought over from Taiwan by Madame Cecilia Chiang, The Mandarin's owner, separates the various dining areas. Heavy-beamed ceilings, an exotic lustrous white Chinese tree set in brilliant blue tile, and a huge Mongolian Fire Pit, around which diners can grill their own delicacies, highlight an atmosphere that is understated but striking.

Madame Chiang has taken elaborate care to reflect the ways of the sophisticated China she knew as a girl in Peking, and she has combined Chinese modern and antique pieces in her restaurant. Similarly, she has achieved a combination of mandarin with modern in her entrees; they are exotically delicious.

SHRIMP BALLS

1 pound shelled, uncooked shrimp, chopped
1/4 pound water chestnuts, chopped finely
1 whole egg
1/2 t salt
Dash pepper
1 t ginger root, mashed
1 fresh scallion (white part only), chopped finely
1 T dry white wine

Mix all the ingredients well. Form into small balls and deep fry in vegetable oil until golden brown. Serve immediately.

Brut Champagne

PRAWNS A LA SZECHWAN

1/2 pound prawns, raw
1/2 t garlic, minced
1/2 ginger root, grated
3 scallions, chopped
1 t dried red chili peppers, chopped very finely
2 T vegetable oil
2 T Sherry
4 T catsup
Pinch of sugar
1 t cornstarch mixed with 2 T water

In a Chinese wok, skillet, or chafing dish, heat oil until quite hot. Saute shrimp, garlic, ginger root, scallions, and chili peppers. Cook for a few minutes. Add Sherry, catsup, and sugar; then add cornstarch mixture to thicken, and continue to cook, stirring constantly, until prawns are done. Serve immediately.

Cold Duck

SWEET AND SOUR SNAPPER

1 red snapper, about 3 pounds
1 egg
8 T sugar
8 T catsup
8 T soy sauce

4 cups vegetable cooking oil
4 T cornstarch
4 T wine vinegar
2 cups water
2 T Sherry

Clean fish, leaving head, tail, and fins intact. Make 6 parallel slashes on both sides so the sauce will soak into the meat. Rub 2 T soy sauce, Sherry, egg, and some dry cornstarch on both sides. Deep-fry the fish, first on one side, then the other, 'til both sides are dark brown but not burned. Remove fish and put it on a long plate. Serve with the following sauce.

Sauce:

Put the catsup, vinegar, sugar, and soy sauce in one pot. Mix and boil a few minutes. Then gradually add the mixture of water with cornstarch and keep stirring

72

until a thick sauce results. Pour the sauce over the hot fish and serve. Decorate with sweet pepper and carrot shreds, if you like.

NOTE: The fish may be deep-fried in advance and refried again just before serving. In this way, the meat will be more crisp.

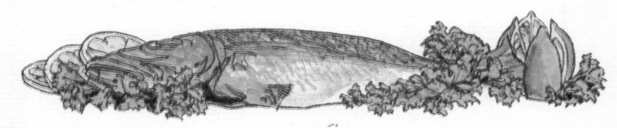

Chablis

STEAMED CRAB WITH GINGER

1 t ginger, peeled and finely chopped
1 T vinegar
1 T brown sugar
1 T soy sauce
2 T dry white wine

Steam live crabs, then scrub and crack them. Serve hot with a dipping sauce made of the ginger, vinegar, brown sugar, soy sauce, and wine.

Some experimentation is advised here, as every Chinese cook has his own proportions.

Serve immediately.

Rose

CRAB MANDARIN

2 T rice wine (or dry Sherry)
1 t vegetable oil
1 T ginger root, crushed
2 T white onions, finely sliced

Saute the cleaned, scrubbed, cracked, and pieced crab with Chinese rice wine (or dry Sherry) in a small amount of vegetable oil in a wok over high heat, together with crushed, peeled ginger, and onions.
Serve immediately.

Dry Sauterne

Sabella & La Torre

If Sabella and La Torre seems more of a family-style restaurant than others along Fisherman's Wharf, it may be because seven members of one family operate this friendly spot. Mike Sabella, co-owner with his brother Frank and nephew, Louis La Torre, likes to reminisce about the early days of the wharf.

"You wouldn't have recognized this place 30 - 40 years ago," he said. "There were crab pots boiling over wood fires — the whole area was filled with smoke and the smell of fish cooking. This street was made up of six fish stands, with white tile counters packed with ice and loaded with all kinds of fish. People used to just buy fish and take it home. When they started to want to eat it here, we opened a small place, and served clams on the half shell, fresh crab, cocktails, and the like."

Over the past quarter-century, Sabella and La Torre has expanded, along with its diners' appetites, into a quality restaurant. An underwater ocean scene adorns one wall, holding the diner's attention while he awaits an entree, always cooked to order, always superbly prepared under the direction of chef Steve McGee.

SHRIMP CREOLE

4 stalks celery, chopped
1 medium onion, chopped
1 clove garlic, chopped
2 T oil
1 t mixed pickling spice
Pinch rosemary
1 t sweet basil

Pinch oregano
1/2 cup water
1 cup tomato puree
1 cup canned whole tomatoes, mashed
1 pound shrimp, cooked and cleaned
1/2 cup Sherry

Saute celery, onion, and garlic in oil until slightly browned. Lower heat and add pickling spice, rosemary, sweet basil, and oregano. Slowly add tomatoes and simmer for a few minutes. Add tomato puree. Bring mixture to a boil, then add shrimp and Sherry. Allow to cook for 1 minute, or until the shrimp have heated through. Serve over steamed rice.

Grenache Rose

SALMON WITH EGG SAUCE

4 salmon steaks
1 T flour
1 T butter
Pinch of salt
1 cup milk
1 t parsley, chopped
4 hard-cooked eggs, chopped
1 t Worcestershire sauce
2 T Sherry

Poach salmon in plain salted water. Drain and place on plate in low-heat oven to keep warm.

Mix flour, butter, and salt in double boiler. When melted, slowly add milk and stir until thick. Add parsley, eggs, Worcestershire sauce, and Sherry. Stir together until well blended and spoon over the warm salmon slices.

Pinot Blanc

CRAB VICTORIA

3 T butter
3 T flour
1 cup chicken broth
1/2 cup cream
8 ounces cheddar cheese, diced
1 can (4 ounce) mushrooms, sliced
3 T Sherry
Salt, pepper, paprika to taste
2 cups crabmeat, flaked

Melt butter in top of double boiler. Stir in flour and gradually add stock and cream. Cook, stirring constantly, until thick. Remove from heat and set over hot water. Add cheese, and stir until cheese melts. Add mushrooms, Sherry, and crab. Let stand over hot water until serving time. Serve on noodles or toast points.

Dry Semillon

OYSTER STEW

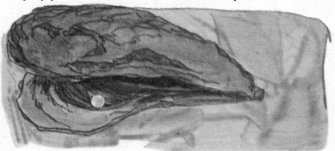

For each person:

6 oysters
2 T butter
6 ounces half-and-half
Pinch of salt and pepper

Melt butter in a shallow pan and saute oysters only until edges curl. Slowly add half-and-half. Add salt and pepper to taste. Serve in a pre-warmed bowl.

Folle Blanche

81

SAND DABS MEUNIERE

2 pounds sand dab fillets
Salt
Pepper
Flour
3 T butter
Juice of 1 lemon
1 T chopped parsley

Sprinkle the fillets lightly with salt and pepper. Dust with flour and brown quickly in a skillet in which 2T butter has been melted. Cook the fillets on each side until golden brown, then remove them to a heated platter. Add the remaining butter, the lemon juice, and parsley. Pour over the fish on the platter and serve.

Chablis

TOMATO STUFFED WITH SHRIMP

2 large firm but ripe tomatoes
1 cup small shrimp, cooked and peeled
1/2 cup celery, diced
1 green onion, chopped
1 T lemon juice
1/2 cup mayonnaise
Dash of salt

Iceberg lettuce, shredded
2 canned artichoke hearts
8 asparagus spears, cooked
2 hard-boiled eggs, quartered
4 ripe olives
1 cup Thousand Island dressing
(see page 152)

Peel tomatoes, hollow out centers with a small spoon, and turn upside-down to drain. Combine shrimp, celery, green onion, lemon juice, and mayonnaise. Place each tomato on a salad plate covered with shredded lettuce. Sprinkle the inside of each tomato with salt. In the hollow of each tomato place an artichoke heart.

Fill the tomatoes with the shrimp mixture, covering the artichoke hearts. Top each tomato with 1/2 cup Thousand Island dressing and 2 ripe olives.

Garnish each serving with 4 asparagus spears and 1 quartered egg.

Rose   83

FILLET OF SOLE STUFFED WITH CRAB

1 T flour
1 T butter
Pinch salt
1 cup milk
1 pound crabmeat
1 T grated cheese
1/2 t Worcestershire sauce
1 t dry mustard
1 T Sherry
Dash Tabasco sauce
8 sole fillets
Paprika
Additional butter and grated cheese

Mix flour, butter, and salt in the top of a double boiler. Set over boiling water. When butter is melted, slowly add milk; stir until thick. Combine crabmeat, 1 T grated cheese, Worcestershire, mustard, Sherry, and Tabasco with enough white sauce to bind. Place a spoonful of mixture on end of each fillet and roll it up.

Place each roll in a buttered baking dish or casserole. Sprinkle fish with 2 additional T of Sherry and cover with remaining white sauce. Sprinkle with more grated cheese, paprika, and dots of butter. Bake for 20 minutes in 375° oven.

Green Hungarian

A. Sabella's

A marquee at the entrance guides the diner to an elevator that whisks him to the third-floor main dining room of Sabella's on Fisherman's Wharf, where floor-to-ceiling windows frame San Francisco's favorite harbor views.

Elegantly appointed in shades of green, gold, and red, with leather banquettes and perfectly set tables, Sabella's is created for the diner's indulgence. And indulge he can, in ordering from one of the more extensive menus on the wharf. Every manner of fish and shellfish is offered, with recommendations of California wines.

After dinner one can repair to the long bar in the other wing, where an elaborate, polished copper-and-brass cappuccino machine dispenses this beverage.

Antone Sabella established the original restaurant in 1920 on this site, replaced in 1964 with the three-story building devoted on the first floor to shops, and on the two upper floors to fine dining. (The second floor is generally available for parties only.) Today, his son, Lucien Sabella, carries on in his father's tradition, serving entrees from recipes handed down through four generations.

TURBOT STUFFED WITH DEVILED CRAB

8 turbot fillets
4 ounces butter
3 whole green onions, chopped
1 1/4 pounds crabmeat
3 ounces Sherry
1 T mustard
Dash cayenne pepper
Dash nutmeg
1/4 T Worcestershire sauce
1 pint half-and-half
1 T (heaping) flour
4 egg yolks, beaten
Melted butter
Sherry
Paprika

90

Melt 4 ounces of butter in a saucepan. Saute the green onions, add crabmeat and saute it slightly. Add 3 ounces Sherry, mustard, cayenne pepper, nutmeg, Worcestershire sauce, and salt; heat until hot. Add cream.

Make a paste of 2 ounces melted butter, and flour. Stir into crab mixture and cook slowly for about 10 minutes, or until smooth and thick. Slowly add egg yolks to mixture and stir well. Remove from heat and allow to stand for a few minutes while you place 4 fillets in a buttered ovenproof casserole. Cover each with the crab stuffing, and top with 4 remaining fillets. Pour a thin stream of melted butter over the top of each and generously sprinkle with a little Sherry. Dust with paprika.

Place in 375° oven and bake for 15 minutes. Serve at once.

Riesling

CALAMARI SAUTE PICCATA

2 large button mushrooms, sliced
1 green onion, minced
1/2 clove garlic, minced
1/4 fresh tomato, peeled and diced
2 T Sherry

1 T lemon juice
Chopped parsley
1 large squid, cleaned
2 T olive oil

Score squid by making several light cuts in a square pattern (not too deep).

Heat olive oil in heavy skillet until hot. Add mushrooms and onions, and cook until tender. Add squid, garlic, and tomato; reduce heat and cook 5 to 7 minutes. Drain any excess oil from pan, turn heat up, and add Sherry. Add lemon juice and allow to simmer for a minute or so.

Serve on a bed of steamed rice and sprinkle with chopped parsley.

Gamay

NEW OYSTERS ROCKEFELLER

24 large oysters, in shell
24 crab legs
6 T butter, melted
Salt and pepper
2 1/2 cups thick, creamed spinach*
1 pound rock salt
Grated Parmesan cheese

*Make this by adding thick
 cream sauce (see page 154)
 to cooked, drained spinach.

    Open oysters and loosen them from shells. Place 6 oysters per person on bed of rock salt in either a pie tin or a flameproof casserole. Brush melted butter on each oyster. Sprinkle lightly with salt and pepper, and place under broiler until oysters begin to curl (about 2 minutes).

    Remove from broiler and place a crab leg on each oyster. Put spinach in pastry bag and pipe on top of each oyster. Sprinkle with Parmesan cheese, and place in hot 375° oven for 10 minutes. Serve immediately.

Chablis

SCALLOPS THERESA

1 1/2 pounds scallops
4 button mushrooms, sliced
2 green onions, chopped
1/2 cube butter
1 cup Mornay Sauce
1 cup spinach in cream sauce (see p. 154)
2 T grated Parmesan cheese
4 scallop serving shells

Mornay Sauce:
1 1/2 cups dairy cream
1/4 cup onion, chopped
2 T butter, melted, and blended with
4 T flour
Dash of nutmeg
3 T grated Parmesan cheese
1 egg yolk, beaten with 2 T cream

For the sauce: Cook first 5 ingredients over low heat 5 minutes, stirring well. Add egg and cheese, and bring mixture just to the boil. Remove from heat.

Saute scallops in butter. Add mushrooms and onions; saute until tender, about 3 minutes. Drain butter. Add Mornay Sauce, simmer 3 minutes. Place spinach in a pastry bag and pipe edges of scallop shells. Place scallop mixture in center of shell, sprinkle with Parmesan cheese, and place in 375° oven for 6 minutes. Serve.

Johannisberg Riesling

Scoma's

Pier 47 on Fisherman's Wharf harbors Scoma's, next to the gulls' perches and the fishing boats' masts. The small intimate restaurant sometimes seems overshadowed by the steamers berthed next to it, but their presence only enhances the mood at Scoma's.

This comparatively new restaurant was founded by brothers Al and Joe Scoma, whose fondness for their mother's cooking is one of the reasons for their success: Many of the specialities and sauces featured are actually prepared from the recipes she brought over from Palermo, Italy. The Calamari Alla Bella Maniera is a favorite dish "prepared in the delightful Sicilian style," according to the menu. We are happy to have the recipe, translated here as Squid in Wine Sauce.

The Lazy Man's Cioppino belies its name, as the sauce for this elegant dish can be made well in advance, then stored in the refrigerator to allow the sauces to "blend." Just minutes before serving, fresh shellfish - oysters, clams, prawns, and crab - can be added to the sauce. This entree is best served with a chilled white wine; at Scoma's the selection is a white Tuscany, bottled in a fish-shaped souvenir.

ABALONE STEAKS

8 abalone steaks, pounded and trimmed	1/4 pound of butter
Flour	Seasoned salt
2 eggs, beaten with a small amount of water	Lemon wedges
Dry bread crumbs	

Sprinkle the abalone slices with seasoned salt and then dip them into flour, egg mixture, and then into dry bread crumbs.

Melt 1/2 of the butter in a skillet and quickly fry each abalone slice no more than 1 1/2 minutes on each side. Be sure to give each slice plenty of room in the skillet, and to add more butter as it is needed. Turn slices only once.

Often abalone slices will curl when fried. To avoid this, slash the edges before breading. If the slices have been properly trimmed however, they do not tend to curl. Properly cooked abalone will be only slightly colored, not brown. Long cooking will toughen the meat and ruin the flavor. Serve hot with lemon quarters.

Chardonnay

GRILLED MAHI MAHI

1 1/2 pounds mahi-mahi steaks
1/4 pound butter
1 t salad oil

1 clove garlic, minced
1 t soy sauce
1 T lemon juice

In a small saucepan melt the butter and saute the minced garlic for one minute. Remove from heat and add oil, soy sauce, and lemon juice. Pour over fish steaks and allow to marinate for 15 minutes.

Broil, turning once, until fish flakes. Serve with lemon slice and sprig of parsley or, if desired, top with Amandine Sauce.

Amandine Sauce: Omit garlic. Quick-fry steaks rather than broiling, but marinate as directed.

After steaks have fried, remove from pan, and to the pan juices add 1 cup chicken broth, 1 T butter and 1 T minced parsley. Allow to heat through. Pour mixture over cooked steaks, and top with sauteed almonds.

Dry Semillon

SQUID IN WINE SAUCE

1/2 cup olive oil
1 clove garlic, minced
1/2 cup green onions, chopped
1/2 cup fresh mushrooms, sliced
1/2 cup white wine (Chablis or sauterne)
1/2 cup tomato sauce
1/4 t salt
1/2 t pepper
3 squid, 8-inches long, cleaned and skinned
Flour
Fat for deep frying

Heat the olive oil in a skillet. Add the garlic, green onions, and mushrooms; saute them lightly. Add the white wine and tomato sauce. Simmer 1/2 hour or longer over a low flame. Add salt and pepper. Meanwhile, dip the squids in flour, and pat off the excess, and deep fry them in hot oil until golden (this happens very quickly). Drain them briefly on paper towels and add them to the simmering sauce. Continue to cook for a short time to blend the flavors (long cooking will toughen the squid). Serve immediately.

TOMATO SAUCE: To a can of tomato sauce (use the size necessary for the number of servings needed), add a bit of chopped onion, minced garlic, a bay leaf, a dash of oregano, a sprinkle of thyme, salt and pepper. Simmer to reduce liquid and blend the flavors for at least 1/2 hour.

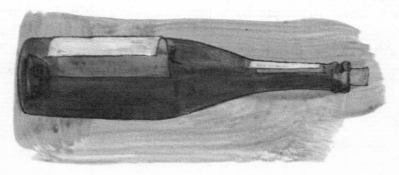

Zinfandel

101

SOLE AMANDINE

2 pounds sole fillets
Salt
Butter
Flour

Juice of 1/2 lemon
2 1/2 cups chicken broth
1 T parsley, chopped
4 ounces sliced almonds, sauteed in butter

Sprinkle the fish fillets lightly with salt, and then dip each one into flour.

Melt about 1/2 a stick of butter in a heavy skillet. Place the fillets in a single layer and cook on a medium-high heat until golden brown on each side.

Repeat until all fillets have been cooked, adding additional butter as needed. (As fillets are cooked, place them on a heatproof platter to keep warm in a slow oven - 200°.) When all have been cooked, mix together 2 T flour, chicken broth, lemon juice, and parsley. Pour this sauce over fish, and top with almonds.

Pinot Chardonnay

SOLE VIA REGGIO

1 pound sole fillets
1/2 onion, chopped
1/2 garlic clove, minced
1/4 pound fresh mushrooms, sliced
Pinch of oregano

1/2 cup white wine
1 T tomato paste
3 T solid-pack tomatoes
1 cup water
1 cup fresh spinach, chopped

Saute onion and garlic in oil for just a minute or two, and then add mushrooms. Allow to saute for 5 minutes at medium heat, and then add: oregano, white wine, tomato paste, 3 T solid-pack tomatoes, and 1 cup water. Cook this basic sauce for approximately 5 minutes.

Place fish in this sauce and continue cooking over low heat for 15 minutes.

A few minutes before serving, add spinach. Allow to heat through, and serve with rice and a vegetable.

Dry Sauterne

LAZY MAN'S CIOPPINO

1/2 onion, chopped
1 garlic clove, minced
1 pinch oregano
1 bay leaf
1 pinch sage
2 cans (No. 2 1/2) solid-pack tomatoes
1 T tomato paste
1/4 cup water
Salt and pepper to taste
1 1/2 pounds crabmeat, cooked
4 large oysters
8 scallops
8 prawns, shelled and deveined

Saute onion and garlic in olive oil until soft. Add spices and allow to cook 5 more minutes. Add tomatoes, tomato paste, water, salt and pepper, and simmer for 1 hour. Strain before using.

When ready to serve, add the seafood to the sauce and cook for about 5 minutes. Serve in bowls with plenty of good sourdough French bread.

The sauce for this dish may be made any time. It can be stored in the refrigerator for several days and will freeze beautifully.

Pinot Chardonnay

SOLE MARGUERY

8 sole fillets
Salt
Cayenne pepper
1/2 cup dry white wine
3 T butter
3 T flour
1 cup chicken broth
1/4 cup grated Parmesan cheese
1/2 pound lobster meat, cooked
1/2 pound small shrimp, cooked
1/2 pound crab legs, cooked
1/2 pound sliced mushrooms, sauteed

Set oven at 350°. In a single layer and in a shallow, buttered baking dish, place fish fillets. Sprinkle lightly with salt and a dash of cayenne. To the side of the fish, slowly pour in the wine. Tightly cover with foil and bake for 15 minutes. Opening one corner of the foil, carefully pour off liquid into a measuring cup. This should be about 1/2 cup. Re-cover fillets and set aside.

In a deep saucepan and on a low heat, melt butter and stir in flour. Add the 1/2 cup reserved liquid and 1 cup of stock or broth slowly; stir until mixture is thick and smooth. Arrange fillets on an overproof platter and pour sauce over them. Sprinkle with grated cheese and top with any or all of the suggested garnishes. Return to oven until cheese melts and sauce is bubbling.

Dry Sauvignon Blanc

Spenger's

When the Spengers first opened their "little country store" in Berkeley, across the Bay from Fisherman's Wharf, at the turn of the century, it was customary to hoist a flag atop the gable when the catch was good. The flag was a signal to the community that fish was fresh at Spenger's that day.

A flag is no longer needed at Spenger's Grotto, for the fish is ALWAYS fresh.

Frank Spenger, Sr., started that little country store as an adjunct to his home, and served crab and shrimp from huge cauldrons out-of-doors, operating a small store from a street-side room. The now famous fish grotto was developed and expanded from this small beginning by the son and grandson of the founder.

The interior maze of rooms harbors sea relics from old and famous ships. The wood paneling is beautiful teak from the old Lurline, and the braces in the dining room and cocktail lounge were once part of San Francisco's old ferry boats and lumber schooners. It is a setting that enhances the superb seafood cuisine at Spenger's, where good food and good wine are the symbols of success.

109

BAKED SALMON CREOLE STYLE

6 salmon fillets
1 cup celery, chopped
1/2 cup onion, chopped
1/4 cup green pepper, chopped
1 can (No. 2 1/2) solid-pack tomatoes

Salt and pepper
MSG
Parmesan cheese
1/4 cup Sauterne

Poach salmon fillets slightly (see page 158) until the rawness disappears, then place them in a casserole and cover with this sauce: Combine celery, onion, green pepper, and tomatoes, and allow them to simmer together for a few minutes. Add salt, pepper, and MSG to taste.

Sprinkle with grated cheese and wine. Bake in a 350° oven until golden brown. Serve with boiled rice.

Cabernet Sauvignon

BARBECUED SWORDFISH

6 swordfish steaks
1/4 cup butter
1 onion, chopped
1 green pepper, chopped
2 T brown sugar
1 T Worcestershire sauce
1 T prepared mustard
1 cup chili sauce
1/2 clove garlic, minced
Dash Tabasco sauce

Sprinkle swordfish steaks with salt and pepper. Combine remaining ingredients and boil slowly for 15 minutes.

Place steaks in broiler pan. Baste with sauce. Broil about 3 inches from the heat. Turn once and baste again. Serve with more of the hot sauce.

Chablis

FISHKABOB

1 1/2 pounds swordfish, cut in cubes
6 slices bacon, cut in half
12 large scallops
6 large prawns
12 small onions
12 slices green pepper
6 mushroom caps
Melted butter for basting

Sherry Sauce:

1/2 cup butter
1/2 cup Sherry
1/4 cup chicken stock
3 T cornstarch

Wrap the swordfish cubes with the bacon, and thread the pieces onto metal skewers, alternating with the other ingredients as follows:

Swordfish - Onion - Scallop - Green Pepper - Prawn - Green Pepper - Onion - Scallop - Swordfish - Onion - Mushroom Cap.

Broil, about 3 inches from heat, turning to brown all sides. Baste with melted butter. When nicely browned serve each skewer on a bed of steamed rice.

Sherry Sauce: Melt butter in saucepan. Add chicken stock and Sherry wine and boil slowly. Thicken with cornstarch. When fishkabob has finished broiling, baste well with the sauce and serve.

White Pinot

FROG LEGS

1 pound of frog legs
Salt and pepper
1 egg
1/2 cup milk
Flour

2 T butter
1/2 small onion, chopped
1/4 cup Sherry
1/4 cup bottled clam juice
Hot fat for deep frying

Arrange frog legs on a board and sprinkle lightly with salt and pepper. Beat egg and milk together. Dip frog legs into egg mixture and then flour. Deep fry in hot fat in a 375° oven 3 to 5 minutes, until deep, golden brown.

Meanwhile saute onion in 2 T butter. Add the Sherry and clam juice. Allow liquid to reduce slightly. Place cooked frog legs on platter and pour the sauce overall. Sliced mushrooms may be added to the sauce at the same time as the onion, if desired. (If the sauce does not thicken enough in reducing, add a small amount of flour mixed with 1 T of wine or clam juice. Add slowly to mixture until thick.)

Riesling

OYSTERS KIRKPATRICK

12 fresh oysters
Butter
6 slices bacon, cut in half, fried
   until crisp and drained
Catsup
Parmesan cheese
Sherry

Open oysters and set them on the half shell in a baking pan filled almost to the top with rock salt. Dot each oyster with a small amount of butter. Broil just until edges begin to curl. Remove pan from broiler. On the top of each oyster place a half-slice bacon, 1T catsup, 1/2 teaspoon Sherry, and sprinkle with Parmesan cheese. Replace under broiler and broil about 2 minutes, or until cheese slightly melts. Serve at once.

Champagne, Natural

SWORDFISH STUFFED WITH LOBSTER

6 slices swordfish
1/2 pound butter
1/2 cup celery, minced
3/4 pound lobster meat, minced
Salt and pepper
1 cup chicken stock
3 eggs

1/2 t poultry seasoning
1 1/2 cups fine bread crumbs
2 cups cream sauce (see page 154)
4 T Parmesan cheese
4 T capers
1/4 cup Sauterne

Cut a pocket into the side of each steak. (Cut from the side but not clear through.) Set aside.

Melt butter in a skillet and saute celery, onion, and lobster for 3 minutes. Add chicken stock, poultry seasoning, salt and pepper. Add bread crumbs and mix thoroughly. Remove from heat. Beat eggs slightly with a fork and add to mixture until it is smooth.

Spoon stuffing into swordfish pocket, reserving a small amount. Spread a thin

116

layer of the stuffing on top of each steak. Place in a buttered pan and broil until brown, then lower the heat to 375° and bake in oven for 25 minutes. (Or until the fish flakes when pricked with a fork.)

Caper Sauce: Saute capers in wine and add to cream sauce. Whip well and set aside. When fish has baked, place it carefully into a casserole. Ladle the caper sauce over the fish, sprinkle with Parmesan cheese, and brown.

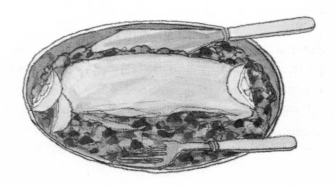

Brut Champagne

SOLE DELICIOSO

3 pounds sole fillets
Shortening
1 cup flour
2 cups bread crumbs
2 eggs
1 t nutmeg
2 T lemon juice

   Combine flour, bread crumbs, and nutmeg. Mix eggs and lemon juice. Dip the sole first into the egg mixture and then into the flour. Fry the fillets quickly (about 3 minutes on each side) in a large skillet in which you have heated about 2 T of shortening. (Add more shortening as needed.) Fish should be well browned. Serve with Tartar Sauce (see page 153).

Rose

RED SNAPPER AMANDINE

3 pounds red snapper fillets
2 cups flour
1/2 cup sliced almonds
6 T butter

2 T lemon juice
1 cup milk
2 eggs

Mix eggs into milk. Roll fish fillets in flour, then dip them in egg and milk mixture, and back into the flour. Sprinkle the slices with salt and pepper. Saute them in hot fat in a large pan. Cook about 5 minutes on each side, or until golden brown.

Almond Sauce: Spread almonds on a cookie sheet and heat them in a moderate oven until golden brown. Melt butter in a saucepan and allow it to brown (be careful not to allow it to burn!). Add lemon juice and browned almonds. Heat one minute, and ladle over fish. Serve hot.

Chablis

Tadich Grill

Years before Fisherman's Wharf became a seafood-restaurant mecca, the Tadich Grill, located a few blocks from the wharf, was a major purveyor of the fruits of the sea. Founded in 1849 in the wholesale district, the Grill established a reputation with the political and mercantile customers which has carried over in time and location to the new locale on California street, where the Buich brothers maintain the long-favored atmosphere of old San Francisco.

A long counter which doubles as the bar runs the length of the restaurant; plain tablecloths loom snowy white against the dark-walnut paneling of the booths. A spotless kitchen at the rear maintains the Grill's original claim of being the "best-equipped Mercantile Lunch Counter in the Wholesale District".

It is traditional to begin a meal at this charming gold-rush vintage eatery with a generous bowl of chowder, and there are two recipes herewith: Coney Island Clam Chowder and Abalone Chowder. The menu, printed daily, contains a wide variety of gourmet entrees which keep this delightful place filled to capacity.

ABALONE CHOWDER

1 pound fresh abalone,
    ground or chopped very finely
1/4 cup butter mixed with 2 T oil
1/2 cup leeks, thinly sliced
1/2 cup onions, chopped
1/2 cup green peppers, chopped
1/4 cup celery, chopped
1/2 pint fish stock or clam juice
2 cups diced potatoes
Salt and pepper to taste

Sauce:
1/4 cup butter
1/2 cup flour
Salt to taste
Pinch of nutmeg
Pinch of cayenne pepper
1 pint half-and-half
1/4 cup Sherry

In a gallon pot, put the oil and butter mix. When mixture is hot, add all of the vegetables and saute them until they are lightly brown.

Add the chopped abalone and the clam juice, and then bring to the boil.

Add the diced potatoes and let the chowder simmer while you prepare the following cream sauce.

In a separate saucepan, melt 1/4 cup butter. Add the flour, then blend it in thoroughly. Add salt to taste, a pinch of nutmeg, and cayenne pepper. Let simmer for 2 minutes.

Now add a heated pint of half-and-half, mixing constantly. When smooth, add Sherry.

Add this cream sauce to the above simmering chowder. Bring to a quick boil, stirring well.

Serve with chunks of fresh sourdough or French bread.

Dry Sauterne

CRAB LEGS SAUTE

2 dozen crab legs
1/4 cup shallots, minced
1 small clove garlic, minced
1/2 cup mushrooms, thinly sliced
1/4 cup Sherry
3 T clarified butter
Salt and pepper to taste

Dry crab legs on a paper towel; dust very lightly with flour.

In a large frying pan, heat the clarified butter. Add the crab legs and saute them until both sides are a very light brown. Add shallots and mushrooms. Saute until the mushrooms are wilted. Add Sherry and cook at a very high heat until the wine is reduced to half. When finished, there should be only a very light brown sauce glazing the crab legs.

Serve with rice sprinkled with parsley.

Riesling

CONEY ISLAND CLAM CHOWDER

4 dozen hard-shell clams
2 ounces salt pork, diced
1/2 cup leeks, thinly sliced
1/2 cup onions, chopped
1/2 cup green peppers, chopped
1/4 cup celery, chopped
3 cups canned tomatoes, crushed
1 quart clam juice
1/4 cup oil and butter, mixed
3 medium potatoes
Salt and pepper to taste

Scrub clams with a brush, then set them in a large kettle. Cover with a quart of water. Steam clams over high heat until their shells open.
(Be sure to discard any clams whose shells are open prior to boiling.)

126

Strain the clams, saving the juice.

Shuck the clams and chop them.

In a gallon pot, heat the oil and butter. When hot, add salt pork, leeks, celery, onions, and peppers; saute them until they are very light brown.

Add the clam juice and the tomatoes and bring to the boil.

Add the diced potatoes and chopped clams; cook until potatoes are done.

Salt and pepper to taste.

Serve with plenty of crackers and butter.

Rose

Tarantino's

Walking into Tarantino's dining room is like arriving at a cinerama theatre with a wide screen, where the show is already in progress. The famed "marine-view" windows overlook boat docks where yachts, party-fishing boats, commercial boats, and all manner of watercraft are tied up. The "screen" is constantly in motion, and the sumptuous surroundings within the restaurant itself are often overlooked - the plush carpeting, the cushy dining chairs, the elegant service - provide an atmosphere of timelessness wherein the major enjoyment is the moment.

Each dish that the restaurant serves is presented with a gourmet touch; whether it be an added sauce or a pinch of seasoning, it is that special something that continues to add to Tarantino's reputation for gourmet cuisine.

The late California state senator Eugene McAteer with his friend, Dan Sweeney, created Tarantino's in 1946, embellishing the basic appeal of the restaurant with huge photographs of early San Francisco which cover the walls, bits of history for the diners to enjoy while reminiscing about the "old days."

CRAB CURRY

1 pound crabmeat
1 apple, peeled and cored
1 small onion, chopped
2 stalks celery
1/4 pound butter

1 cup tomato puree
2 T curry powder
1/4 cup flour
Water

Saute the apple, onion, and celery in butter for about 15 minutes, but do not brown. (You can run these 3 ingredients through a food grinder if you wish.) Then add the flour and the curry powder, which have been mixed together, and continue to cook for about 5 minutes, stirring constantly. Add the tomato puree and enough water to bring the sauce to thickness desired, stirring all the while until smooth. Salt and pepper to taste, and then add cooked crabmeat. Blend thoroughly, being careful not to shred the crabmeat too finely.

Serve hot over rice.

Rose

DEVILED CRAB TARANTINO

1/2 cup cream sauce
1 T Worcestershire sauce
3 T dry mustard
2 T French mustard
1/4 cup pimento, chopped

1 pound crabmeat
Salt and pepper
Butter
Grated Parmesan cheese

Make the cream sauce, following the recipe on page 154 but halving it, and substituting milk for the cream. Bring the cream sauce to a boil, then add the Worcestershire sauce, and the mustard (remember, a little at a time so you can suit your taste). Then add the pimento and crabmeat, folding in the latter so as not to break up the crabmeat. Salt and pepper to taste.

Place in individual casseroles, crab shells, or a large casserole, and sprinkle overall with grated Parmesan cheese and melted butter.

Bake in a 450° oven for 15 to 20 minutes, or until golden brown. Serve hot.

Riesling

SOLE EN PAPILLOTE

1 pound fresh sole fillets
Salt and pepper
2 ounces white wine
1/4 pound fresh mushrooms, chopped
3 small green onions, chopped
1 kernel shallot, minced
1 cup thick cream sauce
Parchment paper

Cut each fillet of sole into 4 pieces. Roll each piece lengthwise and secure the roll with a toothpick. Place the rolls in a saucepan and cover with water. Add salt and pepper to taste and 2 ounces of dry white wine; simmer gently 10 minutes or until done.

Chop the mushrooms, onions, and shallot finely, and add to 1 cup of rich cream sauce (see page 154) in the top of a double boiler. Thin the cream sauce

132

down a little with stock from the sole, and cook for 5 minutes.

Put each of the sole fillets on a heart-shaped parchment paper, and divide the sauce among them. Then fold the paper over and crimp the edges, sealing all the way around. Place the paper-enclosed fillets on a pie tin and bake in a 400° oven for 4 minutes, or until the paper is puffed up. Serve in the paper on a hot plate.

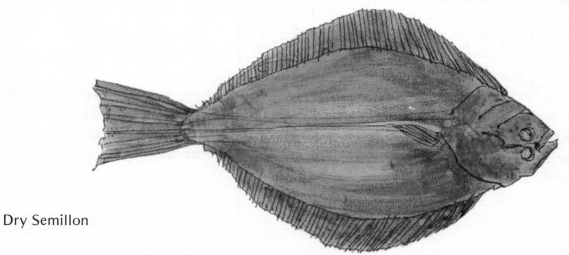

Dry Semillon

OYSTERS TARANTINO (individual serving)

6 oysters on the half shell
2 T spinach, finely chopped
1 green onion, finely chopped
1 t grated Parmesan cheese

1/2 cup cream sauce (see page 154)
2 T white wine
1 egg yolk

Place cream sauce in pan, then add spinach, green onion, grated cheese, white wine, salt and pepper to taste. Bring to a rolling boil, stirring constantly. Then beat in egg yolk while sauce is boiling (if one yolk is not sufficient to make sauce stand heaped on a spoon, use two).

Put six mounds of rock salt in a pie tin and put deep side of oyster shell in salt, so it will not tip. Then put each oyster in its shell and heap sauce over each, sprinkle grated Parmesan cheese on top and drizzle with melted butter.

Bake in a 450° oven until golden brown. Serve hot with quartered lemon.

Folle Blanche

HALIBUT FLORENTINE

2 pounds halibut steak fillets
1/2 cup white wine
Juice of 3 lemons
1 cup heavy cream sauce (see page 154)
8 ounces spinach, cooked and chopped

3 green onions, finely chopped
Salt and pepper
3 egg yolks
1/2 cup grated Italian cheese

Place halibut in shallow saucepan. Cover with water; add wine and lemon juice. Boil 5 to 10 minutes or until liquid is reduced to one-third. Remove halibut; place in baking dish.

Place cream sauce in second saucepan, and add broth from halibut. Then add spinach, onions, salt and pepper. Mix and bring to a boil. Remove from fire and stir in egg yolks.

Pour this sauce over halibut and sprinkle with grated cheese.

Bake at 400° until golden brown.

Serve from baking dish.

Chablis

Toro's

From a land south of the Border comes the atmosphere in Toro's, where Spanish music sets the scene. Cowhides cover rugged, handmade chairs, with more hides hanging above brilliant orange tiles that band the large room. From the center of the high ceiling hangs a huge chandelier, a combination of black wrought iron and imported glass squares that is said to weigh over a ton.

Chatting with Tony Winston, owner-manager of Toro's, one could easily imagine his icy blue eyes scanning the far horizon from the bow of a brigantine bound for a new land. Actually, however, Tony has for years designed and decorated restaurants for other people. About four years ago he decided it was time he designed one of his own. Toro's is the unique result.

The spotless kitchen in the center of the dining room is a model of efficiency, where the service is almost instantaneous, and the food is cooked to order - fish and chips, several varieties of beef 'burgers, tasty tacos, and a seafood plate. Tony's wife contributed her special party favorites to our collection.

FISH 'N' CHIPS

4 medium-sized potatoes, cut in strips
2 pounds haddock fillets
1 1/2 cups prepared pancake flour
1/2 t salt

1 1/4 cups water or milk
Fat for frying
Malt vinegar
  (place on table for optional use)

Peel potatoes, then cut them into strips. Cut fillets into serving pieces. Mix pancake flour, salt, and water until blended. (If you are doing this at home it is a good idea to deep fry all of the potatoes at once and keep them warm in a heated oven while you deep-fry the fish. Or you could borrow your neighbor's deep-fat fryer for the night and cook the potatoes and the fish at the same time.)

Fry potatoes in hot, deep fat (375°) 3 to 5 minutes or until golden brown. They seem to fry better if soaked in ice water for a short time, and then are blotted dry before deep-frying. As potatoes cook, dip the well-dried haddock strips into batter. As the potatoes are finished, drop the fish into the deep fat and fry for 4 minutes, or until deep brown. Drain all on absorbent paper before serving.

Chablis

TROUT VERONIQUE

4 fillets of trout
1 1/2 cups dry white wine
1 1/2 cups chicken broth
3 T butter
3 T flour

1 t salt
1/4 t cayenne pepper
1 1/2 cups light cream
1 cup seedless white grapes
1 1/2 cups Hollandaise Sauce (see page 154)

In a deep skillet arrange the fillets. Add wine and chicken broth. Bring to a boil and cook over low heat about 7 minutes or until fish flakes. Transfer fish to a heated platter. Allow liquid in the skillet to reduce on medium heat.

Melt butter in a saucepan and blend in flour, salt, and cayenne pepper. Gradually add the cream, stirring constantly. Mixture will be very thick. Thin with 1/2 cup of broth from cooked fish (use more if needed). When sauce is smooth and thick, allow to cook slowly over low heat for 5 minutes. Remove from heat and fold in Hollandaise Sauce. Spoon grapes, then sauce over fish.

Place under the broiler for 2 minutes, garnish with fresh grapes, and serve.

Traminer

MARINATED PRAWNS

3 pounds large prawns, cooked and cleaned
1 cup olive oil
2 cups white or wine vinegar
1 large onion, peeled and sliced
3 carrots, peeled and sliced (parboiled slightly
   in salted, boiling water)
4 cloves garlic, peeled and sliced
Pinch oregano
Dash salt and pepper
6 whole chiles
1 can ripe olives
Parsley

Put olive oil in a large clay or enamel pan over medium heat. Saute half of the onion and 2 cloves of garlic until brown. Remove and discard. Lower heat slightly, and carefully add vinegar, remaining garlic, onions, chiles, and carrots. Let come to a boil. Remove from heat and allow to cool. Add the prawns, and bring to the boil. Remove from heat and allow prawns to cool in the liquid.

Prepare this dish a day or two in advance for a more concentrated flavor. Drain the prawns before serving in a chilled bowl, garnished with ripe olives and parsley.

Emerald Dry Riesling

ROLLO DE PESCADO

6 fillets of sole
3 plain omelets, very thin and cut in half
6 sticks (2 inches x 1/2 inch) Monterey Jack cheese
1/2 cup sliced pimento-stuffed olives
1/2 small can green chiles, chopped

2 T chopped parsley
3 green onions, chopped
Salt and pepper

SAUCE

1 large can peeled tomatoes
1 lemon, thinly sliced with skin intact
1/2 cup onions, finely chopped
1/2 t oregano
1/2 can green chiles, chopped
1 cup chicken broth

Prepare omelets: Thin omelets are made by beating 2 eggs with 2 teaspoons water. Pour 1/3 of total amount into a heated 6-inch skillet in which a small amount of butter has been melted. Tip skillet, allowing egg mixture to spread evenly over bottom of pan. This procedure takes only a few seconds. Cook only until omelet is lightly browned underneath and dry and shiny on top. Repeat procedure twice, adding more butter to the skillet as needed.

On top of each raw fish fillet place one omelet half, then one stick of cheese, and a little of each of the next four ingredients. Sprinkle with salt and pepper and roll. Secure fish with toothpicks. Place in refrigerator.

Brown onion in butter until golden brown, add tomatoes and simmer slowly until rich in color and slightly thickened. Add oregano, chiles, and broth and cook about 10 more minutes.

Arrange fish rolls in buttered oven dish, and pour the sauce over all. Top with lemon slices, cover with foil and bake in 350° oven for 35 minutes.

Garnish with pickled onion slices and parsley.

Sylvaner

143

Pompei's Grotto

Huge boiling pots of crab adorn the exterior of Pompei's Grotto, extending a subtle, aromatic invitation to enter this small, family-style cafe on the wharf's bordering Jefferson Street. One step up and you're in a cozy bar, presided over more often than not by the owner, Frank Pompei, unless he's in the kitchen overseeing the dinner preparations, as he's done for over 25 years.

Nouveau curtains made of beads, and checkered tablecloths, plus the addition of a well-stocked bar, have given this restaurant a recent face-lifting from its previous quarter-century reputation as a crabpot stop-and-serve spot. Mr. Pompei's staff is well known for its excellent service. Old-time customers from as far away as Dallas and New York make the Grotto a must stop during their visits to the City.

Mr. Pompei likes to serve a great variety of seafood specialties, among which whitebait and crab Louis rank high. He also serves whole crabs with the Louis dressing featured in the following recipes, or with oil and vinegar, red sauce, or mayonnaise. And, of course, crab <u>au naturel</u> is always a favorite.

CRAB LOUIS

1 pint catsup
1 pint mayonnaise
1 t garlic salt
1 t horseradish
Chopped hard-boiled egg
Fresh crabmeat

Iceberg lettuce
Lemon wedges
Black olives
Tomatoes, quartered
Hard-boiled eggs

Blend ingredients well, chill and serve generously atop fresh crabmeat that has been spread over a bed of chopped iceberg lettuce on an oval platter. Garnish with lemon wedges, black olives, quarters of tomatoes, and more hard-boiled eggs.

This one-quart portion of sauce can be stored in the refrigerator for future use with any kind of seafood salad.

Pinot Blanc

DEEP-FRIED PRAWNS

1 1/2 pounds large raw prawns
Hot fat
Batter

Batter:
1/4 t salt
2 eggs
1/2 t lemon juice
2 t water

Clean and butterfly fresh prawns. (To butterfly prawns, cut down length of the back on rounded side with a sharp knife. Lift out sand vein with knife tip, leaving the tails on to use as handles when dipping in batter.) Place cleaned prawns on paper towels to dry thoroughly. Dip the prawns into the batter, and drop into hot deep fat. Fry 3 to 4 minutes or until golden brown.

Place cooked prawns in a basket lined with paper towels to drain slightly before serving.

BATTER: Beat the eggs until fluffy and then add the salt, water, and lemon juice.

Chablis

147

SOLE MEUNIERE

2 pounds sole fillets
Salt
Flour
Butter
Juice of 1 lemon
Chopped parsley

Sprinkle the fish fillets lightly with salt and then dip each one into the flour. Melt about 1/2 cube butter in a heavy skillet. Place the fillets in a single layer and cook on a medium-high heat until golden brown on each side. Repeat until all fillets have been cooked, adding additional butter as needed. As fillets are cooked, place on a heatproof platter to keep warm in a slow oven (200°).

When all have been cooked, squeeze the lemon juice into the liquid in the pan and pour it over the fish. Sprinkle with parsley and serve immediately.

Traminer

WHITEBAIT

1 pound whitebait
Salt
White pepper
Flour
Hot fat (370°)

Wash the whitebait thoroughly and dry carefully in a clean cloth. Sprinkle with salt and white pepper, and roll in flour. Shake off extra flour and drop into deep-fry basket. Whitebait are so small they cook in 1 to 3 minutes, so watch carefully.

Serve with wedges of lemon and Tartar Sauce (see page 153).

Sylvaner

THE LEGEND OF THE HANGTOWN FRY

One of the most legendary dishes on Fisherman's Wharf is Hangtown Fry. The many versions of its origination make one wonder if any one of them is true. One point they all seem to agree on is the point of origination, that being Hangtown now known as Placerville, California.

One of the tales I've been told is of a highly successful miner having gold to burn going in to town to show off his good fortune and also to have a decent meal. In order to achieve both goals at once, he walked into a Hangtown restaurant and loudly ordered the three most expensive things on the menu. They were oysters, bacon, and eggs.

Another version is much the same but it tells of the gentleman of dubious character having been convicted of a crime. In order to stall for time, when asked what he would like for his last meal he named Hangtown Fry, explaining it was a mixture of bacon, eggs, and Olympia oysters. By the time the tiny oysters arrived from Puget Sound, two states away, the condemned man's cohorts had rescued him.

150

HANGTOWN FRY

1 cup oysters (cut large ones into quarters)
1/2 cup flour
3 eggs, slightly beaten
4 t water
1/2 cup fine bread crumbs (or corn meal)
4 strips bacon
1/4 t salt
Dash of black pepper

Roll the oysters in flour, then in the beaten eggs that have been diluted with the water, and then in the bread crumbs.

Using an 8 inch skillet, fry the bacon until it is crisp. Remove the bacon and drain off some of the fat. Add the oysters and brown them quickly. Replace the bacon. Over this pour the remaining egg mixture. Salt and pepper to taste. Cook until underside is firm. If top is not firm, place under broiler until slightly brown.

Zinfandel Rose

SAUCES

THOUSAND ISLAND DRESSING

1 1/2 cups mayonnaise
1/2 cup bottled chili sauce
2 whole green onions, chopped
1 t capers
4 gherkins, chopped
1 t parsley, chopped
1 t green pepper, chopped
1/2 t paprika
1 hard-boiled egg, grated

152

Combine all ingredients. Chill well.

TARTAR SAUCE

1 1/2 cups mayonnaise
1 T parsley, chopped
1 clove garlic, minced
1 t capers, chopped
5 sweet gherkins, chopped
1/2 t tarragon vinegar
1/4 t white pepper

Combine ingredients and serve with any broiled or fried fish.

CREAM SAUCE

1 T butter, melted
1 T flour
1/2 t salt
Dash cayenne pepper
1 cup milk

Blend flour, salt, and pepper with the melted butter. Gradually add milk. When mixture is smooth, stir over medium heat until it thickens. Cook 5 minutes over low heat. Makes 1 cup.
Thick Sauce: Use 4 T butter, 4 T flour

FISH STOCK

Heads and trimmings of 2 white fish
1 carrot, scrubbed and sliced
2 onions, sliced
1 bay leaf
2 white peppercorns
Water to cover (add wine if desired)

Wash the fish debris, discarding any discolored skin.
Combine all ingredients in enameled pan and bring to the boil. Simmer for at least 1 hour. Strain.

154

COURT BOUILLON

2 quarts cold water
3/4 cup red or white wine
2 carrots, scrubbed and sliced
2 onions, sliced
1 bay leaf
1 sprig thyme
2 whole cloves
1 t salt
4 peppercorns

Combine all ingredients; bring to the boil. Lower heat and simmer for 1 hour. Liquid is now ready to poach any fish.

Many people believe this is the only way to treat a fish, as it is convenient and allows the full flavor of the fish to remain in the meat.

HOLLANDAISE SAUCE

2 egg yolks
1 T lemon juice
Salt and cayenne pepper to taste
1/4 pound butter, melted

Place first 3 ingredients in a blender container. Run on low speed 5 seconds. Pour butter in steady stream, blending at same speed just until sauce is thickened.

155

GENERAL INFORMATION FOR BUYING AND PREPARING FISH

There is no proof that eating seafood will make you more intelligent. There is, however, definite scientific evidence that it is a smart idea to include fish and shellfish in your diet if you are interested in enjoying a healthy and vigorous life.

For instance, did you know that fish is one of the four basic foods? It is rich in proteins, vitamins, and minerals; it's low in calories, and, best of all, most of the fat in fish is polyunsaturated. There is no doubt of the nutritional excellence of fish, so plan to include it in your diet often. Aside from the fact that it is good for you, it tastes good too!

When buying fish, be sure to choose only those with clear eyes—full and not sunken. Watch for broken skin or discolored traces in the flesh, which flesh should be elastic and firm enough to not leave a mark when pressed with the finger. The fish should have a clean and pleasant smell.

Ask the fish dealer to clean and trim the fish for you, leaving them whole or filleted, as you desire. He probably has had years of practice and can do a far better job and a faster one than you. However, do remember to ask him for the head,

157

skin, and bones if you are going to make a fish stock.

If fish is the main dish for the meal you are planning, you will need about 6 ounces per serving for fillets and steaks. If the fish is large and bony, 9 ounces per person would be about right. With lobster and large prawns, plan on 10 to 12 ounces per person, and lobster tails call for a one-to-one ratio.

Fish should be cooked as soon as possible after purchase. If necessary to keep it overnight, place it in a covered container, or wrap it in aluminum foil and store it in the coldest spot of your refrigerator.

Poached or fried fish is usually served WITH a sauce.

Baked or stewed fish is usually prepared IN a sauce.

Never confuse the word "poach" with "boil." Fish should never be boiled unless it is to make a soup of some kind; then the flavor should be boiled out into the liquid in which it has been cooked.

In poaching, the fish is placed in a kettle and covered with a prepared and cooled court bouillon. The second it comes to a boil, the heat must be lowered until the liquid is gently simmering. Most fish take from 7 to 10 minutes for every 2 pounds from the time the liquid comes to a boil.

When frying a fish, remember—the smaller the fish, the higher the heat. If the fish is large and thick, the heat must be lower for a more gradual penetration of the flesh.

ABALONE

A rather ear-shaped shell houses the abalone. Its foot-like muscle that clings to the rocks is the edible part. Without the shell it is creamy white on top and gray at the base. The best way to remove abalone from the shell is to use a long, sharp, thin-bladed knife. Run the tip of the knife around the edge of the abalone between the meat and the shell. Keep the blade as close to the shell as possible. Force the knife blade around and under the meat until the meat falls from the shell.

Now clean and trim any dark portions from the meat, and you are ready to

159

begin pounding. If the abalone is to be fried, cut it into slices with a long-bladed knife. You can put the meat through a food chopper if you don't care to tenderize it, then use it for fritters or chowder.

The greatest problem to cooking abalone is the proper pounding of the meat. A wooden mallet, rolling pin, or wooden potato masher is best for this chore. Hit the slices of abalone with a steady motion, and lightly. If you hit too hard you will end up with a limp mass. If you don't pound it hard enough you may bite into tough pieces after it is cooked. When it has been pounded properly, it should feel soft and velvety and look something like a thick breakfast pancake.

CLAMS

It is said the Pilgrim Fathers referred to clams as "those little treasures hidden in the sand." They are very nourishing and should be used regularly in making up the family menus, as they are available and in season all year 'round.

There are varieties beyond belief but for the most part, there are the hard-shell or littlenecked clam, the soft-shell or long-neck clam, and razor clams.

Hard-shell are from the Atlantic Coast, the smallest of which are called cherrystones. These are good served raw on the half shell, in cocktails, steamed, or broiled.

Soft-shells are found in both the Atlantic and the Pacific. They are excellent for clam bakes, frying, steaming, roasting, and for broth.

The razor clam, which got its name because it somewhat resembles an old-fashioned razor, is found along the Pacific Coast, and is used mostly minced and in chowders.

HOW TO PREPARE CLAMS: Clams may be bought live in the shell by the dozen or bushel. They are alive if their shells hold tightly together. It is said that if the live clams are placed in a shallow pan with enough water to cover and then sprinkled with dry cornmeal it helps to clean out any sand as well as whiten the meat. In order for this to be done correctly the clams and cornmeal must stand for several hours, or overnight. This step is not absolutely necessary, however. If you scrub and rinse the clams well before using them, you will rarely have a problem with sand.

Insert a strong, sharp, slender knife between the shells and cut around the clam through the muscle, then twist to pry open. Drain the clams, or drop both meat and juice into a bowl. At that time, if it seems necessary, rinse the meat in several waters to get rid of grit.

There is a thin skin or film that covers the body of the soft-shell and razor clams and this should be removed before cooking. If live clams have been steamed to open the shell and are not to be eaten at once, remove the meat as quickly as possible and cool it in cold water. If this is not done the meat will tend to be tough when used.

CLAMS AT THEIR BEST: Use hard-shell clams. Wash and scrub with a stiff-bristled brush, rinsing several times. Place in a deep kettle that has a tight-fitting cover. Pour in a small amount of water, cover, and allow to steam until shells open. This will not take very long, so do not overcook! Pile a dozen in each individual soup bowl and serve to guests. Be sure to furnish a large empty bowl for the shells. It is sacrilegious to serve this dish with anything more than melted or drawn butter. The broth remaining in the steamer should be served in cups to accompany the clams.

DRAWN BUTTER: Melt 1/4 cup butter, add 3 T of flour mixed with a dash of cayenne pepper and 1/2 t salt. Gradually add 1 1/2 cups hot water, stirring constantly. When smooth, allow to boil 5 minutes and then add another 1/4 cup butter, a bit at a time.

CRAB

Of the many, many species of crab found all over the world, the most commonly known for sweetness of taste are the blue crab of Chesapeake Bay, the Atlantic and Gulf Coasts; the larger Dungeness crab of the Pacific Coast, and the

Alaskan King Crab.

Any variety of crab may be either soft-shell or hard-shell. All crab is hard-shell in its ordinary state, but as the crab grows, it must enlarge its shell. As it does this, that is—when it sheds the smaller shell, it takes two or three days for the new shell to harden. If the crab is caught during the "in-between" period it is known as a soft-shell crab and is considered a delicacy among crab aficionados.

Crabs can be purchased alive, although most markets sell fresh crab meat by the pound also. When choosing a crab, pick one that is heavy, weight-wise, in proportion to its size. If a crab is very light it may prove to be practically hollow; large ones may be tough and the small crab will have little meat.

HOW TO PREPARE CRAB: It is easier said than done, but I will say it anyway. If you are dealing with a live crab, scrub it as best you can in cold water. Make certain at the outset that Mr. Crab knows "who's boss"—that he is the one who will end up in hot water!

The scrubbed crab should be dropped into boiling, salted water and allowed to boil for 10 to 15 minutes. Remove and cool. Pull off the claws and legs and crack the shells with a nutcracker or a hammer. Crack the claws from any side, but the leg joints are cracked more easily along the narrow edges. Break off the segment that folds under the body from the rear. Hold the crab in the left hand, the back toward you, and slip the fingers of your right hand under the top shell. Now, pull the body downward, without breaking it. This releases the top shell. After you have removed the top shell, hold the body under the faucet and remove

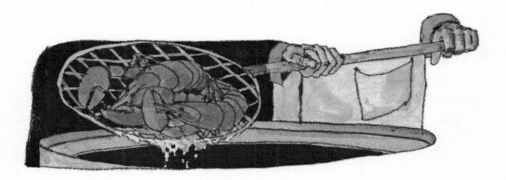

the digestive tract and gills. The gills are easily recognized as feather-like, spongy tissue which can easily be removed with the fingers. Make a split along the central crease and then hold half of the body in your left hand. With a sharp knife cut the hard membranous covering along the outside edge. It is now easy to remove the tender sweet meat in each cavity with a nutpick or one of the crab's own sharp claws.

CRAB AT ITS BEST: After it has been boiled, serve crab cleaned, cracked, and in all its glorious sweetness! A nice touch is to have a small dish of homemade mayonnaise to dip the luscious morsels into.

LOBSTER

The delicate, tasty meat of lobster makes it a favorite among those who appreciate fine cuisine. It is rich in energy-giving glycogen which makes it nutritious too. Lobsters are available all year long but are most plentiful in summer when they come closer to shore and are more easily caught.

Deep-ocean lobsters, caught by means of traps during the dead of winter in deeper waters, are available all year long. When the inshore lobsters cease to feed and the normal supply dwindles, the deep-ocean lobster continues to feed and is trapped because of a more constant water condition.

A lobster is dark green with red specks when alive but after cooking it is a bright red. Two types are marketed, the North Atlantic variety that has large claws, and a southern cousin from Florida or California, which does not have claws but has two large antennae protruding from the head.

HOW TO PREPARE LOBSTER: After plunging the live lobster head first into salted, boiling water, cover the pot and allow it to boil 20 to 30 minutes, depending on the size of the lobster. Remove lobsters and lay them on their claws to drain. When they have cooled enough to handle, do the following.

1. Twist off the claws.
2. Crack each claw with a nutcracker or hammer.
3. Separate the tailpiece from the body by arching the back until it cracks.
4. Bend back the flipper and break it off the tailpiece.
5. Insert a fork where the flippers broke off, and push the meat out.
6. Unhinge the back from the body. (The green liver is a delicacy.)
7. Open the remaining part of the body by cracking it apart sideways.
8. The small claws may be placed in the mouth and the meat sucked out.
9. Be careful not to mix the feathery particles under the shell with the meat.

LOBSTER AT ITS BEST: Lobster is most delicious served cold, just after it has been boiled, with a lemon-flavored mayonnaise. Many prefer buying just the tail part, frozen, and serving it broiled. It is a simple matter to allow the lobster tail to thaw, brush it with a basting sauce of butter, lemon juice, a dash of Worcestershire sauce, salt and cayenne, and broil about 4 inches from the flame for

168

8 to 10 minutes. Turn and broil about 6 to 8 minutes on the other side, then turn again, baste again, and allow to finish cooking (2 or 3 minutes). Serve on a platter garnished with lemon slices and parsley.

OYSTERS

Oysters are highly prized as a food because of their flavor. However, they should be considered from the standpoint of their high food value and ease of digestibility. Their composition is similar to that of milk, which makes them rich in vitamin and mineral content. They also contain carbohydrates not usually found in so-called "flesh foods," and it is this carbohydrate in the form known as glycogen that allows oysters to be so easily digested. They are even more easily digested raw than when cooked.

Aside from the nutritional standpoint, oysters have great appeal to the thrifty homemaker because they are 100% edible. You could not ask for anything easier to prepare: just open and serve! Of course they are delicious baked, broiled, fried, stewed, you name it; if it contains oysters, it will be good. One thing must be remembered, however: Never cook oysters too long. They are not actually "cooked"—just heated through enough to leave them plump and tender, retaining their delicate and distinctive flavor.

In past years there has been a belief that oysters should only be eaten during months that have an "R" in them. It is a myth. It came from the fact that oysters are not supposed to be a desirable food during the summer-months' spawning season. Admittedly, they are not as tasty if eaten at that time but they are not dangerous. Also, the fact that spawning season is at different times in different localities means oysters are now obtainable in prime quality every month of the year.

HOW TO PREPARE OYSTERS: Be sure to keep oysters at a cool temperature until ready to use, and do not open them any sooner than necessary. Scrub the shells with a stiff brush and cold water. Hold the deep half of the shell in one hand, which should be protected by a heavy glove. Insert the point of a thin, sharp knife between the shells just back of the hinge at the pointed end of the oyster and cut through the large muscle that holds the shells together. It is then a simple matter to separate the shells and loosen the oyster meat, taking care not to spill any of the liquid contained in the shell. It has an exquisite flavor and should be enjoyed together with the meat of the oyster no matter what method of preparation you have chosen.

OYSTERS AT THEIR BEST: Serve them in the deep halves of their shells on a bed of crushed ice surrounding a small glass containing a sauce. Garnish with lemon wedges and sprigs of parsley. Six to a portion is usually correct.

SHRIMP

Shrimp are the most popular crustacean in the United States. They abound in most of the coastal waters of the United States, but the main producing areas are the Gulf of Mexico and the Pacific Coast.

Grayish-green in color and small and slender in size, shrimp turn a bright pink when cooked. They vary in size, but an average shrimp is about 3 inches in length and there are 20 to 40 shrimp to the pound.

Prawns are similar to shrimp in color and shape but they are much larger. They may be easily interchanged with any recipe calling for shrimp.

When shrimp are packed in ice for shipment, their heads have been removed and they are uncooked. Referred to as "green" shrimp, they may be purchased this way. Most fish markets and supermarkets also sell them cooked, peeled, and ready to eat.

HOW TO PREPARE SHRIMP: Wash as many shrimp as desired in cold water. Drop them into boiling, salted water (1/2 T per quart) and cook from 3 to 8 minutes or until they begin to rise to the surface. Long cooking will give shrimp a rubbery texture and toughen them. Drain and cool. Tear each shell open from the underside of the shrimp from the head toward the tail. Then with a sharp-pointed knife, remove the black sand vein visible just under the surface of the shrimp. One pound of cooked shrimp should provide you with 6 generous portions.

SHRIMP AT THEIR BEST: Make a cocktail sauce of 1 cup of bottled chili sauce, 2 T lemon juice, 1/4 t salt, 1/2 t Worcestershire sauce, 1/2 t horseradish, and a dash of Tabasco. Combine all ingredients, chill, and pour over cooked and cleaned shrimp in a serving dish. Garnish with a slice of fresh lemon and serve with oyster crackers. Provide a small fork for each individual serving.

RECIPE INDEX